ABOVE ALL THINGS

ABOVE
❧ ALL ☙
THINGS

*The Journey of an Evangelical Christian
Mother and Her Gay Daughter*

SHARI JOHNSON

CHANGING LIVES PRESS

CHANGING LIVES PRESS
50 Public Square #1600
Cleveland, OH 44113
www.changinglivespress.com

Unless otherwise stated, scriptures taken from the HOLY BIBLE, NEW INTERNATIONAL VERSION®. Copyright © 1973, 1978, 1984 by International Bible Society. Used by permission of Zondervan Publishing House. All rights reserved.

The "NIV" and "New International Version" trademarks are registered in the United States Patent and Trademark Office by International Bible Society. Use of either trademark requires the permission of International Bible Society.

"Scripture quotations taken from the Amplified® Bible, copyright © 1954, 1958, 1962, 1964, 1965, 1987 by The Lockman Foundation. Used by permission." (www.Lockman.org)

Excerpt from *The Power Within* copyright © 2012 by Changing Lives Press used by permission of the publisher.

Library of Congress Cataloging-in-Publication Data is available through the Library of Congress.

ISBN-13: 978-0985024-80-2
ISBN-10: 09850248-0-1

Cover and interior design: Gary A. Rosenberg • www.thebookcouple.com

Printed in the United States of America

10   9   8   7   6   5   4   3   2   1

Contents

This book is dedicated to the Lesbian, Gay,
Bisexual and Transgender community.
I pray that you will be able to accept
my sincerest apologies and love.

Introduction

*I*f you are looking for a book that will support your particular side of the controversial gay issue, this isn't it. However, if you are the parent, child, former spouse, relative, friend, or co-worker of someone who is Lesbian, Gay, Bisexual, or Transgender and you are confused or hurting, this book was written with you in mind. If you fit into one of the categories above but would not read a book like this on a bet because you already know everything there is to know about this subject and no one is going to change your mind, this book is written especially for you—because I was just like you.

To give you a little background, I accepted Jesus Christ as my personal savior in 1971. A friend of mine was a new Christian and she wanted to share the good news with me. I didn't want to hear the good news and thought she had turned into a religious fanatic. I avoided her—until I was getting my second divorce. Jane and I had been good friends, so I felt I owed it to her to let her know. She invited me to her house and I was at such a low point in my life that

I needed someone to sympathize with me, so I went. Instead of patting my shoulder and telling me that everything would be okay, she started talking to me about Jesus—only this time I was listening. I knew that I had managed to screw up my life pretty well by that time, and I was only 28. I am eternally grateful to Jane for not giving up on me.

My church background was Heinz 57. My family didn't go to church, so when I went it was with friends and it was mainly for social reasons. My birth father's family was Irish Catholic, but my parents divorced when I was nine months old. I was able to forgo my senior year of high school and go on to college. I attended a Catholic college for women for a summer and a fall semester, and connected with my Catholic roots. My first husband was Catholic but when he and I got a divorce, it didn't set well with the Catholic Church.

It wasn't too long after accepting Christ when I met James, a divorced man and now my husband of almost 40 years. His was the first divorce in a Pentecostal, Assembly of God family. We attended AG churches until the year 2000. Actually, we did more than attend—church was our whole life. You've heard the saying "They were there every time the church doors were open"? That was our family. I taught Sunday school, Children's Church, Missionettes (a ministry to young girls in the Assemblies of God churches); James taught the Royal Rangers (a ministry for young boys— James called them the Royal Rowdies) and James and I were youth sponsors (these were the days before Youth Pastors). Since the "youth" cleaned the church for fundraising, you probably have an idea of who cleaned the church. We were both involved in ministries for men and for women, and our kids were involved in all the programs available for them as well.

We raised our kids according to scripture and Christian authors. The joke at home was, "Look out—Mom's reading another James Dobson book!"

In 1980, I was asked to start a drama ministry in our large church in Denver, Colorado. I wrote, directed, performed, and produced Christian drama for the next twenty-two years in Colorado, New Mexico, and Texas. (My husband works in the oil industry, so he was transferred often.) I was a drama major at one time—before I realized I would rather eat than act and decided that being a dental hygienist would be more lucrative. However, I felt that God gave me the desire of my heart as a ministry. I was (and still am) a believer in drama as a source of teaching and ministry. There was a lot of humor in my writing to cause people to laugh at themselves and see the error of their ways. (I've never thought that beating people up with the Bible was all that effective.) Many of the dramas were evangelistic in nature, and some were three act plays, passion plays (the story of the crucifixion and resurrection of Christ), and dramatized cantatas. For years, every Christmas and Easter season involved presenting some large dramatic production. James was a big help with the technical part—not my area of expertise.

My purpose in telling you all this is two-fold. First, I want you to have a picture of the type of home that my daughter, Cholene, grew up in—and why it was so difficult for her to come to terms with her sexuality. Second, it will give you an idea of why it was so difficult for me to come to terms with her sexuality.

Cholene chose the title of this book—*Above All Things.* It couldn't be more appropriate. Above all things, there is love. It ranks above teachings, sermons, biases, bigotry, hate, politics and judging one another. But most important, it is *the* most important thing to God—that we love Him, and that we love each other.

The book is written experientially. It is our journey, our story—the story of an evangelical Christian mother and a gay daughter. It is sometimes heartbreaking, sometimes humorous, but always honest.

The original plan was that my daughter and I would co-author this book; sort of my story and her story. Cholene's busy schedule, first as a commercial airline pilot and now as a medical school student, has precluded that plan. She is still weighing in between the covers of this book, just not as much as I had hoped. I suspect that another reason she has not been able to write her story here is that she feels it would hurt me too much to read of her pain—especially since I was a source of much of that pain. I understand how she feels, as I was afraid of hurting her by writing of my struggle when she told me she was gay. It was something I didn't want her to know.

When I first learned that Cholene was gay, I floundered. The only thing I knew for certain was that I loved this child of mine fiercely, and nothing was going to change that.

Prior to this time, I thought I had all the answers. Now

I'm not even sure that I understand the questions. I viewed life as being either black or white—there was no gray. I avoided anyone who didn't think as I did; I was a *my-mind-is-made-up-don't-confuse-me-with-facts* type of person.

This book is written chronologically, as I have lived it. My thinking at the beginning of this journey was much different from my thinking now, and that's a good thing! I have learned a lot about myself throughout this process, but I've learned even more about God. The top three on the list are: 1) God is sovereign. 2) That thing about loving your neighbor as yourself is not a suggestion—He means it, and we don't get to choose the neighbor. 3) God shows up in the most unexpected places.

Although it is written from a Christian's perspective, this book is not written to Christians only. It is my intention and belief that anyone who is embroiled in this issue can benefit from my experience. Too many families and relationships have been torn apart needlessly.

Many names have been changed in this book to protect those who could be hurt by loss of their jobs, loss of their relationships, and in extreme cases, loss of their lives. Unbelievable in this, the twenty-first century, isn't it?

I have often said since starting on this journey that change will come about one heart at a time—and that only God can change a heart. I know this to be true because He changed mine.

CHAPTER 1

The Call

It's true. A single phone call can alter your life. It's also true that a date can be indelibly printed on your mind—even the minds of the history-challenged. It was the evening of July 15, 2002, when my daughter Cholene called to tell me that she was gay. She was thirty-seven years old at the time.

You are probably thinking that surely I had suspected something by this point. Not a clue—I was stunned.

Cholene is an amazing woman who has accomplished things others only dream of doing. My good friend Edwina and I joke about how we want to be our daughters when we grow up—not only because they are accomplished, intelligent, and lovely, but also because they are kind, caring, and compassionate. When I would tell someone about Cholene attending the Air Force Academy, her years as a U-2 pilot, or her job as a captain for United Airlines, I would invariably get the question, "Is she married?" I would say no, along with my stock answer that she had two long-term relationships that didn't work out. Then I would laugh and say,

"What male ego can survive a woman like this?" I would often get a nod and a smile, but because of rampant stereotypical assumptions, I felt they were thinking, "Oh yeah—she's gay." I would want to scream, "Just because a woman can do things better than most men doesn't mean she's a lesbian!"

When Cholene was three years old, she decided she wasn't going to wear dresses anymore and when she was four, she renamed herself "Tom." Actually, it was "Boss Bat Tom," because that was during her *vampire bat* period. She had seen a soap opera at the babysitter's house that had something to do with vampires. She was convinced that a bat had flown in her bedroom window, bit her on the neck, and now she was a vampire bat too. Her dad and I were divorced and his fiancé made her a black cape with her new name emblazoned on the back in large, white letters. Did I rush her off to a child psychologist? No, I thought she was wonderfully creative. She still is. However, she hardly ever wears the black cape any more.

I didn't take her refusal to wear dresses nearly as well. I loved dolls when I was a kid, and loved dressing them up. When Cholene was born, I was delighted to have a little girl, and I thought it would be like dressing up a real, live doll of my own. Alas, it was not to be. Her wardrobe consisted of tee shirts, jeans and black, high-top tennis shoes. She also had no interest in dolls whatsoever. As she grew older, her refusal to wear dresses grew stronger. There was a battle before church every Sunday because *by golly, she was not going to make me look bad by not wearing a dress! What would people think?* I didn't insist that she wear dresses to school, except for one disastrous Valentine's Day when Cholene was a sixth grader. In *my day*, the Valentine's Day party was a big deal. We girls dressed up in pretty pink or red dresses, and I was sure that hadn't changed through the years. I bought her a red corduroy jumper and she was going to wear it to the party or else. I was asked to provide some refreshments, and when I walked into her classroom carrying the cupcakes I had made (pink, white, and red frosting, of course), lo and behold, all the girls were wearing jeans and sweatshirts. Except for the scowl on her face, Cholene looked lovely in her red jumper. She walked over to me, crossed her arms and said, "You happy?" It finally dawned on me that she was a great kid just the way she was. Why would I want her to be any different? Why would I risk causing her to become rebellious and defiant, or make her feel that she didn't measure up to my expectations, or cause her to question herself and her choices—all over the ridiculous issue of clothing? These days the buzz phrase, "pick your battles," would apply. I also had to admit that it was more about protecting my image than it was about her.

Do I think that every little girl who doesn't like to wear dresses or play with dolls or would rather have a boy's name is gay? No, I do not. My stepdaughter Laron is not gay and she fits that same criteria. She's a grandmother now and she still prefers working in jeans and steel-toed boots.

Cholene's call that night was bittersweet. She read a letter to me that she had written as an assignment for a course she was taking in personal development. She was quite emotional—very unusual for her. She said that she loved me and other wonderful things I had wanted to hear for so long. Cholene and I weren't estranged, but there was definitely a strain in our relationship, and it had been there for several years. I wasn't sure why. I thought it might have to do with the poor relationship I had with my own mother—that it trickled down, so to speak. (I had read plenty on the subject.) Or, I thought it might be because of my resentment for Cholene's father. We had a difficult marriage and our divorce was worse. We divorced when Cholene was three years old. I managed to remain angry for years, even after his death—*especially* after his death. (I read plenty on that subject as well.) Cholene was at the Air Force Academy when her father died, and I felt that she would have preferred I were the one who died. She seemed to withdraw and not want me to be a part of her life any more. I didn't want to put her in the position of *duty visits*. I never looked forward to visiting my mother; it was something I *had* to do. I was always overjoyed to hear from Cholene, but I didn't feel comfortable in initiating the contact. I'm sure this was a result of my own fear of rejection—something that had plagued me for most of my life. Cholene was very ill in 2000 and it took a call from a friend of hers telling me how serious the situation was before I got on a plane and flew to New York. I was waiting to hear from Cholene that she needed me. I didn't want to *intrude* in her life. It opened my eyes to how really sick I was—what kind of a mother would not take the initiative to go immediately to her sick child?

She read on, with a great deal of difficulty, that she had

a "different sexual preference." I didn't need to ask her what she meant. I felt like the air had been knocked out of me and that I might never be able to breathe again. I tried not to convey this to her, or the fact that I was crying. It was difficult for her to say and difficult for me to hear. We talked for a long time. The message I wanted to get across to her was that I loved her—no matter what, I loved her. But I also told her, as gently as possible, that I wouldn't be marching in any gay parades and that she knew my thinking on this subject. She pressed me and said, "No. What do you mean?" I couldn't quite believe that she didn't know what I meant. She had grown up in a church denomination that takes a strong stand against homosexuality—we both had heard the same teaching. Cholene excelled in debate, both in high school and at the Air Force Academy, and I have never been a match for her in this department; I knew she was pressing me to take a stand. I struggled for what seemed to me a very long time. My kids joke about how I am honest to a fault. I have been known to carry it to extremes, but honesty and integrity are very important to me. Could I lay down all that I believed and lie to her? I couldn't. I finally said, "It's wrong."

Looking back at that time, if there is one thing I could delete, it would be that one statement. Years later when we were having an e-mail discussion about this book, I told her that I was afraid of being brutally honest because I didn't want to risk hurting her. This was her e-mail response: "The night I 'came out to you,' you were crying (or holding it back, actually). You said that you loved me and then said, 'Of course you know what I think about this.' I knew what you were not saying: It's wrong—it's a sin. A part of me was going to let this pass and move on with the conversation, but I decided not to let it pass. I said to myself, No, I want her to say what she really thinks. I need to know for sure. And so I asked, 'No. What do you mean?' There was a pause. A long pause. You seemed to be struggling with the words that would mean you were announcing the damnation of your daughter to an eternal hell. You were honest about your belief and 'came out with it.' You said in a quiet and serious tone, 'It's wrong.' I did not react or cry or feel anything in particular except that I knew how you felt and that was that. I tried to disconnect emotionally and save it for a time when I could deal with the statement more easily.

"I am telling you this so you will know that in my mind, nothing you could write about my being gay would have as much impact on me as that statement you made that first night. The words, 'It's wrong' embodied the genesis of my lifetime of self-loathing. I have been liberated from that and perhaps together we can liberate others."

During the course of our conversation, my mind was in overdrive, trying to find a reason for why this had happened to her. I began mentally beating myself up, thinking it was my fault. I had frustrated her and somehow had *turned* her when she was a child by not letting her be who she needed to be.

I thought about my three marriages. I must have *turned* her against men because I set such a poor example. I thought she was afraid to commit to a relationship because it would just end in unhappiness and divorce, as mine had. (My third marriage was of almost 30 years duration at this time, but I wasn't thinking too clearly.)

However, uppermost on my mind was something so devastating that I had never been able to tell her. I felt it would destroy her if she knew, and that she would hate me.

It was toward the end of my first year of a two-year dental hygiene program at the University of New Mexico when I discovered I was pregnant. I was married, but my marriage wasn't stable. I knew I needed to finish the program—the day would probably come when I would need to support myself and our son, Chip, who was not quite two years old at the time. Thankfully, this was in 1964—before abortion was legal in the United States. I thought having another child at this point in my life was the worst thing that could happen. I felt I wouldn't be able to finish college and I would be *stuck*. How could I support two children as a single mother, if it came to that? I was desperate. A friend told me about two possible solutions: one was a coat hanger (I don't need to be more descriptive, I'm sure), and the other was jumping off a high place—like a dresser. The idea of the coat hanger was abhorrent, but I decided to try leaping off the dresser. I tried several times, but nothing happened. I finally decided that whatever will be, will be. Besides, I felt like an idiot. Cholene was born during Christmas break of my last year in the program, and I didn't miss a beat. I graduated with my class, passed the New Mexico State Board and became a registered dental hygienist when Cholene was six months old. My worrying was for naught.

I managed to bury this so deeply it didn't surface until I was reading a book nearly twenty-eight years later about how events and choices in our past could affect our present relationships. I thought about the strain between Cholene and me, and decided that this was the cause—the fact that I had tried to deny her life, and that she must have felt that rejection from the womb. My husband and I were both reading in bed, and I read him the passage about how important it was to go to the person you have wronged and set things right, even if they weren't aware of the problem. I started crying and told James what I had done. I said, "I have to call Cholene and tell her." To which he lovingly responded, "Are you out of your mind? Throw that book in the trash!" For once, I did what he told me.

Years later, I volunteered for Birthright, a crisis pregnancy center. Even though I had not been able to tell anyone but James what I had done, I was able to tell precious women and girls who were at that same point of desperation where I was in 1964. I told them what the world would have missed if I had denied this amazing woman—my daughter—life.

My heart was pounding as Cholene and I were talking, and I knew I had to tell her. I was convinced that she indeed had felt rejected in the womb, and that I was the cause of her being gay. I prefaced it by telling her I had something important to tell her and that I was so very sorry that I had done this to her. We had both cried off and on throughout the conversation, but at this point, I was on the verge of losing it. After I told her everything, including my leap off the dresser, there was a brief silence, and then she started laughing. I thought she must be hysterical. When I realized that she wasn't, I said, "Cholene this is serious! You have no idea how I have agonized over this."

She said, "I'm sorry, Mom, but I was just thinking—it's no wonder that I am most comfortable flying at 70,000 feet!"

You just have to love a kid like this. With her one short comment, Cholene exonerated me from years of tormenting guilt.

CHAPTER 2

The Aftermath

After Cholene's call, the first thing I knew I had to do was tell James, my husband. I dreaded it.

James and I married when Cholene was eight years old and my son Chip was ten. James had three children—Laron eleven, Phillip ten, and Jeffery five. Phillip lived with us, but at that time, Laron and Jeff lived with their mother. A year later, Jason came along and completed the "ours" segment of "yours, mine, and ours." (These were the days before "blended family" was a popular term.) Confused? You may have to return to this section if you get lost later. To quote Charles Dickens, "It was the best of times, it was the worst of times."

James couldn't have been more proud of Cholene if she had been his own daughter. He had been in the navy and he loved talking with her about the military, airplanes, politics, and current events. I felt like the *odd man out* more than once. He bragged about her to anyone who would listen. I was afraid that was about to change.

I feel I need to interject something here: Throughout

this journey, I have continually short-changed people and made judgments about how Cholene's being gay will be received. James was the first, but I have done the same with our other children, with my family, with my friends, and with my church; it's the reason it was so hard for me to tell anyone about it. I wanted to protect her. I couldn't stand for anyone to think of her as anyone other than the wonderful person she is. I had to do a lot of soul-searching about this, concerning my motive. Was this another "red jumper" incident? Was I just worried about what people were going to think of me? I can state honestly that it was not. I think most parents feel as I do—we would rather be the ones to suffer than see our children hurt.

Something I could not get out of my mind for months after Cholene's call involved a tragedy that had taken place in San Francisco, California, in 2001. A woman had been attacked and killed by two dogs in the hallway of her apartment building. There was public outrage—until it was reported that the woman was a lesbian. The attitude then seemed to change and conversations went something like this:

"Did you hear about the woman who was mauled and killed by two dogs in San Francisco?"

"Yes. I heard she was a lesbian."

"Oh." That "Oh," spoke volumes. It said, in essence, that she was "inferior," that her death didn't have the same impact as that of another person. The reason this tragedy stuck in my mind was because, God forgive me, I had had fleeting, similar thoughts of my own. One has to wonder why it was even reported that she was a lesbian. What possible bearing did that have on anything?

In 1997, I studied sign language at a college for the deaf, although degenerative arthritis in my hand prevented me from becoming an interpreter. One of my professors, a brilliant woman with a Ph.D. who had been profoundly deaf since the age of three, caused by spinal meningitis, through an interpreter, made a point I will never forget. "Why do people say, 'She is smart, *but* she is deaf.' Why don't they instead say, 'She is smart *and* she is deaf.' Saying 'but' negates the fact that she is smart."

In Cholene's book, *Through the Eye of the Storm,* she refers to the concept of "less than." We sometimes feel we are *less than* (or inferior) to someone else. Or, as in the case of the woman who was attacked, we might feel that someone is *less than* we are. Although I wasn't aware of the term at the time, that was the embodiment of my fear — that people would think Cholene was *less than* because of her sexual identity. And why would I think that? Because I had been guilty of thinking the same thing about others.

James was in the den watching television. I'm sure it took only one look at me to know that something major had just happened. He turned off the TV. James normally is slow to react; he likes to process information slowly and think about something before acting upon it. In cooking terms, he is a crock-pot, while I am a microwave oven. It's one of those "opposites attract" things, but it works well for us. James is 6'4" and weighs 220 pounds, but he has a tender heart and is not afraid to display emotion. It's one of the reasons I love him. His tears didn't surprise me, but I was shocked by what came next. He was all action and said, "Well, I'm going to call her and tell her that she isn't that way!"

When Cholene was a little girl, there was a time when she wanted to go live with her dad. James and I felt it was because she thought she could help him; that it was up to her to help him stop drinking. Even from the time Cholene was a child, she has put the needs and comfort of others above her own. James couldn't stand by and let this happen, so he took it upon himself to have a talk with her. I don't know what he said, but I am sure it was something about it not being her responsibility, and she never went to live with her dad. He thought he could *fix* this also.

I told James he couldn't call her—that it had taken enormous courage for her to tell us, and she would feel that we weren't accepting this—that we weren't accepting her. Instead of talking about what each of us was feeling and sharing our pain, we withdrew from each other and tried to deal with it in our own way. In all the years James and I have been married, we have never gotten the *communication* thing right. A pastor asked me one time if James and I communicated. I told him that I did, but James didn't. He said, "You may be doing a lot of talking, but you aren't communicating." I was shocked (and a little angry) at the time, but I had to admit that he was right. I could talk about surface issues, but I could not get to the crux of the real problem. I did this in all of my relationships. I guess I felt that if I told someone the truth of what was on my mind and heart I would be rejected. James usually shuts down and doesn't let me know his thoughts or feelings either. I think he feels that if we don't discuss it, it will eventually go away. I knew where James stood on the homosexual issue and I felt he would reject Cholene because of that—and because she was his stepdaughter, not his flesh and blood. Even though our opinions of homosexuality were very similar, Cholene was my daughter. All my motherly instincts kicked in and I was a lioness protecting her cub. I was having enough of a struggle—I wasn't about to hear anything negative from him.

James told me some time after this that he had spoken with our son Jason during this time and said to him, "I don't know what to do about this." Jason's answer was, "Dad, it's not up to you to do anything."

As far as my *dealing* with it was concerned, I wasn't. I couldn't get through the day without crying—not once, but several times. My sense of humor has served me well through the years, but it failed me. The best way I can describe it is that it felt like the light had gone out in my life. I read something about joy during this time and noted it in my journal. "Joy equals energy. When I have lost my joy, I have lost my energy. Children have boundless energy—but they also have boundless joy." That certainly explained my lack of energy, but I seemed powerless to do anything about it.

My one ray of hope was from something Cholene told me the night she called—she wasn't currently in a relationship. I thought it wouldn't be any different from unmarried heterosexuals who abstain from sex and remain celibate. I hung on to that and prayed constantly that she would "come out" of this.

21

A day or two after Cholene's call, my son Jason called.

"How are you doing, Mom?"

"Oh, fine." I swear—if I were being held at gunpoint and one of our children called and asked how I was, I would say, "Oh, fine."

"She called me, Mom."

I couldn't say anything for a minute; I was so taken aback by this. Then I told him that I had not wanted to tell him—I was afraid he would feel that the hero had fallen. As the youngest in a family of six kids, Jason had some hard acts to follow. I often thought he might feel that he didn't measure up. Now the silence was on the other end of the line. Then I could hear him crying.

"How can you say that, Mom? I love Cholene. She *is* my hero. I have always loved her and I will always love her." We were both crying by this point.

I told him that I would honor the choice she had made. He said, "Mom, no one would make this choice—it is too difficult. Regardless of what (a Christian leader) says, it is not a choice!" In those few words, Jason made me question what I had believed to that point. Indeed, why would anyone "choose" a lifestyle that could adversely affect her career, her relationships, and close doors in her face that were previously open to her? Even the term "lifestyle" connotes that it is a choice.

I think Jason understood this well. He was not a jock in school, although at 6'4" he could have made any high school basketball coach happy. Unlike his three older brothers and his father, he wasn't interested in playing sports.

Jason is a very talented actor, albeit an undiscovered one. He took a lot of flak in high school from people who thought he was gay. Of course that might have been because he was going through his "I want to be a female impersonator when I grow up" phase.

Again, I was, as Cholene would say, "making a story." I had *spun* the story in my mind that Jason was going to feel vindicated by the news that Cholene was gay—she wasn't perfect after all. I have a very active imagination, which came in handy in the twenty-two years that I wrote Christian drama. However, I have a tendency to take quantum leaps, "fill in the blanks," and come to conclusions that have very little to do with fact. I should probably go into politics. The Biblical term for this is "vain imaginings."

Jason has been an example to me of someone who is comfortable in his own skin and lets others be who they are. Sometimes that has proven to be embarrassing for his dad and me. We were able to get back at him for those times when we wore sandwich signs to his high school graduation. James' sign said, "No, Jason is not adopted." Mine said, "But thanks for asking." He has been on my case more than once for being condemning, judgmental, and intolerant. Of course, I didn't see myself that way at all. I preferred to think that I was "discerning." He and Cholene both have ragged on me for placing too much importance on appearance.

I think God let me experience something that made me wonder if they just might be right. One day Jason came to the dental office where I worked to take me to lunch. I wasn't quite ready, so he waited in the reception room. Jason's taste in clothes has always been a mystery to me. That day he was dressed in the usual weird attire, and had some sort of bandana wrapped around his hair, which I think was probably blue at the time—his hair, not the bandana. I guess Jason reaped the benefit of my epiphany over Cholene and the red jumper—or maybe I was getting too old to fight the clothing battle, but clothes just didn't seem to be such a big deal to me anymore. As I entered the reception area to tell him I was ready, I noticed a well-dressed patient sitting there also. She was pretending to read a magazine, but she was stealing glances at Jason. She had an expression on her face that indicated she might have smelled something disgusting. Now, my son may not have always looked like a fashion plate, but by Jove, he was clean! My first thought, after the one about wanting to scratch her eyes out, was, "Am I like that?" As hard as it was for me to admit, the answer was yes.

Because "appearances" play such a huge role in whether parents accept or reject their child's homosexuality, Cholene asked me to include my experience with this issue in this book.

Appearances were everything when I was growing up. My mother was consumed with looks—hers, mine, and everyone else's. She reminded me constantly that I fell short of acceptable. Unfortunately, regardless of whether the hurtful things she said to me were true had nothing to do with my believing them; someone I loved had told me they were true.

To compensate for my feelings of inferiority I developed

a self-deprecating type of humor. I found that it was less painful if I made fun of my shortcomings before anyone else did. It gave me a semblance of control, rather than my having to be a victim. Nevertheless, I found it nearly impossible to accept a compliment. The best advice I ever received on the subject of accepting compliments graciously came from a dentist I worked for shortly after getting my New Mexico dental hygienist's license. His private office was right next to my treatment room, separated by a sliding wooden door, and he would often eavesdrop on my conversations with the patients. After a patient was dismissed, I would hear the dreaded, grating sound of that door slide open and my stomach would start churning. I knew he would be coming in to set me straight on something I may have misspoken—and, according to him, I rarely said anything right. One day a patient complimented me on my hairstyle, and I went through my usual litany of reasons why that couldn't be true. Sure enough, I had said the wrong thing. After the patient left, here he came. This time he said, "When someone compliments you, say 'thank you' and shut up!" It is still difficult for me to accept a compliment, but I always think of his words and try to heed them.

Mother's attacks and comments on my appearance continued through the years, but the focus changed. It eventually became a matter of my needing a facelift, which she started harassing me about when I was thirty-eight. There was a turn-around in 2002 with the onset of her dementia and she not only stopped criticizing me, she actually began to compliment me. (She probably thought I was someone else.) Even so, the damage had been done. My fear of her criticism was so imbedded that before going to the nursing home to see her I would carefully do my hair and make-up and deliberated over what to wear.

Do I think that my mother purposed to destroy my self-esteem? I thought that at one time, although I now know that she fought demons of her own from her unhappy childhood, and I think that I was just a casualty of that war. But because of my experience and the lack of self-confidence, the inferiority complex and the paralyzing fears of rejection and criticism it caused, I was determined that my kids would grow up differently. Cholene's call threatened that. I knew if it came out that Cholene was gay, she was going to be criticized and rejected. I just couldn't let that happen to her. Even though it wasn't a case of "how is this going to make me look," I still felt that anyone who criticized her or rejected her was doing the same to me. The *appearance* demons were alive and well.

CHAPTER 3

Whose Fault Is It?

I was obsessed with finding a reason for Cholene's homosexuality. I remembered a friend telling me that her father had sexually molested her sister when she was a child, and now that sister was gay. I got it in my head that Cholene had been molested when she was a little girl while visiting her dad. I didn't think her dad had molested her, but I wasn't sure about the men who hung around with him. I asked her during one of our conversations if this had been the case, and she assured me that it was not.

I fixated on Cholene's dad as the cause. As I said before, I became pregnant with Cholene while attending college. Until I finished school, our son, Chip, and I lived in Albuquerque and my husband lived in Española with his mother. Whenever he was drinking, he would go into a rage and say that the baby I was carrying was not his. I realize now it was a matter of transference of guilt, but I didn't understand that at the time. He made it clear that he wanted another boy, so when Cholene was born I felt that he rejected us both. I thought Cholene might have felt this rejection also, and that was the reason she endeavored to accomplish all the things a son would do—trying to win her father's love and favor.

As I was driving to work one morning, just a few weeks after Cholene's call, I tuned in a favorite Christian radio program. The guest was an "expert" on the subject of homosexuality. I was all ears. He had a lot to say, but the part that got my attention was when he said gay men are always a result of a poor relationship with their fathers. Yes! I was vindicated. *I just knew it was her father's fault.* At the very end of the program, the host asked him, "And what about lesbians? Is it their mothers?" The guest replied that yes, it was always due to a bad relationship with their mothers. I felt like someone had punched me in the gut. I became nearly hysterical, sobbing and saying, "Oh dear God—it's my fault! It's my fault!"

For days, I went over every moment of Cholene's life I could remember, trying to find anything I did that might have caused this. I didn't discuss any of this with Cholene. Because things had been rather strained and formal between us for years, I wasn't comfortable with asking her questions about her private life. The long-term relationships I mentioned previously had lasted a total of seven years, and James and I never met either of them. I'm sure distance was one of the contributing factors, but I still felt that Cholene didn't want me to ask her any questions. However, I have to take responsibility in this also because I have an aversion to *prying*. I detest having anyone pry into my affairs, and therefore I dislike asking personal questions of others. After Cholene's original call, she and I spoke on the telephone often. It was always loving and cordial, but we had reached a sort of "don't ask, don't tell" policy of our own. We were talking, but we weren't communicating. We both probably had hurts and questions, but we weren't voicing them. I sank deeper and deeper into the morass.

Finally, probably because he was living with a crazy woman and he needed some relief, James convinced me that the "expert" was wrong. I was able to put it behind me and move on, but I learned some things from this experience:

- Whenever I hear the words "always" and "never" from an *expert,* I run like the wind.

- God is not as concerned about our *beliefs* as he is about our *attitudes.*

- I was not going to be able to rely on my former support systems in the Christian world to get me through this. They are fallible, just as I am.

- My answers are not going to come from the experts. I admit that I don't know the answers, but neither do they. There is only one *expert* when it comes to humanity—the One who created us. (And don't you know He rues the day?)

I was not willing to tell very many people about Cho-lene. One reason was because of the "less than" concept mentioned before, but also because I didn't want people feeling sorry for me. This was not about me. I have never had any patience with a victim mentality, and I certainly didn't want to appear to be one. I told a few close friends, and especially those who have gay children. I had prayed with them and cried with them when they heard about their kids, and I wanted them to know that we were in this thing together. Although I loved them, loved their kids and sympathized with them, it became a whole new ballgame when it was *my* daughter.

I couldn't bring myself to tell my three stepchildren until the following Easter. I wrote each of them a letter. Chip and Jason had been great about it, but I wasn't sure about the bond among step-siblings. Again, I had *made stories.* Phillip has two daughters and I was afraid that he and his wife Cheryl would think Cholene would be a bad influence. I never thought for one minute that Cholene would *recruit* anyone, but because I had bought into that stereotype in the past, I transferred my own prejudice to Phillip and Cheryl. Jeff is a football coach and teacher, and since he leans to the conservative side, I assumed he would have the same mind-set that so many conservatives have—the same one I had for so long. I really didn't think Laron would have a problem with it, but, just as I had feared from Jason, I was afraid they would all see her as a fallen hero. All of our kids are successful in life and I am enormously proud of all of them. Cholene downplays her accomplishments to everyone, and is uncomfortable when anyone brags on her. I have often said she could listen to a crop-duster pilot for thirty minutes, genuinely impressed with what he does for a living, and never mention that she has been a U-2 pilot or a captain of a major airline. She is the same way with the family. However, it is pretty obvious that she has accomplished more than the average bear. Laron responded immediately with a beautiful, loving, and supportive letter. I did not hear from the boys. The stories in my mind continued and grew. I was told a long time after this that they just didn't think there was anything to discuss. They loved her, it didn't make a difference to them, so what's to talk about? MEN! Of course they loved her—I knew that. What was I thinking? As I said before, I continually short-changed people.

During this time, I was teaching a weekly Bible study at Mission Messiah, a Bible-based program for women in crisis. Some of the women have been addicts, some prostitutes, some are there for a last chance before being sent to prison, and some are there because they have been abused by life. I felt that I was empty and that I didn't have anything left to give. I was a mess—how could I possibly help anyone else? I planned to resign.

I try to take daily walks. Not only does it help me to remain healthy, but it's my praying time as well. However, my prayer time had become more of a whining session. I was walking one morning, thinking about how I was going to go about telling the couple who started this amazing ministry that I was resigning. More important, what reason was I going to give? Then something came to mind I hadn't thought about in years. While our children were still living at home, whenever our church needed host homes for young people who were traveling through town with a choir, a drama group, or ministry team, our kids would always volunteer our home. I guess they figured a few more weren't going to make much difference. Next, I immediately thought about my son Chip. When he was a young, unmarried youth pastor in Provo, Utah, the women in the church took care of him. They baked for him, hemmed his pants, invited him to dinner (and he was a picky eater, so that said a lot), and provided a home environment for him to go to if he felt homesick. I then felt that God spoke to me. Now don't freak out when I say, "God spoke to me." It's not as if I hear a booming voice out of Heaven calling my name—although anything is possible. In my case, it's more a matter of a thought that hasn't been there before, and it is usually contrary to the way I normally think. My thinking tends to line up more with the *other* guy. I have heard various people describe how God speaks to them, and He is usually sweet and compassionate. With me He uses more of a, "Straighten up and fly right" approach. However, probably due to my fragile emotional state at this point, He was very gentle.

This is what I felt He was saying: *You took care of other mothers' children when you let them stay in your home, so other mothers cared for Chip when he needed someone. Take care of my daughters at Mission Messiah, and I will take care of yours.*

I didn't resign, and it was through Mission Messiah that I started on my own road to recovery.

CHAPTER 4

Secrets Destroy

Mission Messiah usually runs at full capacity. The women are allowed to keep their children with them, which is one of the reasons why this particular program is so successful. Oddly enough, shortly after I made my "deal" with God, the population was reduced to two women and five children. This was unprecedented in the history of this ministry. I think God provided a little one-on-one (or two-on-one), and I wasn't the one doing the ministering. Because of the intimacy of this small group and because I loved these women and trusted them implicitly, I found myself telling them about Cholene. I did not feel comfortable telling people from the Christian community at large, but I was baring my soul to these women who were relatively new in the faith.

Why was that? I have already stated that I was wrong to prejudge the people in my church, but it was more than that. Why was my first thought that Cholene would be judged and hurt by Christians? I think it is because we have missed the message of God's love—perhaps not the one that

He loves us, but the one that He also loves those who aren't like us. I was made aware of this while I was editing Cholene's book, *Through the Eye of the Storm*. She quotes my son Chip as saying, "If you have to believe as I do in order for me to serve you, then I am not a servant." When I read that, it hit me dead center. I had been guilty of avoiding anyone who didn't think as I did—politically or spiritually. I transferred my own prejudices to all other Christians. A friend told me recently of something she read on a bumper sticker (a source of wisdom second only to refrigerator magnets). It was a quote by Mohandas Gandhi: "I like your Christ, I do not like your Christians. Your Christians are so unlike your Christ." A very sad commentary indeed.

After I told Sharon and Theresa about Cholene, they reached out to me with love and compassion, totally without condemnation or judgment. Sharon recommended that I see a volunteer at Mission Messiah who had counseled her. I have never been one to go to counselors—professional or otherwise, but I knew I needed some "outside" help. I told Sharon I would call this woman. As I was driving home from Mission Messiah that day, I felt *lighter* than I had in a long time. Then two words came to my mind, "Secrets destroy." I knew God was telling me that I had to turn loose of the death grip I had on this, or it was going to destroy me. I thought about situations where people have a secret in their past and their lives are overshadowed by the fear that someone will find out. I didn't want to live that way.

I guess Sharon didn't trust me to follow through—and with good reason—so she had the counselor call me. When

I met with Betty, even though I told her about Cholene, she instead focused on my problems with relationships—my erecting a "wall" to insulate myself, or walking away from a relationship rather than risk being hurt. I was an inveterate people pleaser. As I have said, I had an obsessive fear of rejection and I felt inferior and insecure. I have often joked about the difference between my son Chip, whose self-esteem is quite healthy, and me. If I know someone doesn't like me I say, "They don't like me. What's wrong with me?" If someone doesn't like Chip he says, "They don't like me. What's wrong with them?"

Betty quickly zeroed in on the source of my problem—my mother; or rather, my perception of my relationship with her. Prior to this, I had never heard the term Theophostic Healing. It is a process used in therapy for healing emotional pain found in traumatic memories. It sheds God's light (Theophostic) on the lies we have believed about ourselves. Betty asked me to remember a particularly traumatic incident concerning my mother, but she didn't ask me to tell her what it was. Then she prayed and simply asked Jesus to show me the truth in that memory. He did. The result was amazing. Because I am a Christian and Christians are not supposed to hate their mothers (!) I had given lip service to forgiving my mother for years. But I knew in my heart that I had not. In a matter of a few minutes, it was a done deal—it was over. It had not been about me at all. It was about my mother and her emotional pain and sickness. I have had further, in-depth Theophostic healing since then, but my mother was not the topic. As I said, it was a done deal. Still, I could not risk telling her I had forgiven her. I was afraid she would turn it back on me, telling me that she had done nothing to hurt me and that she should be the one forgiving me.

Since starting this book, my mother has passed away. Four years after my session with Betty, I received a call from the nursing home telling me that my mother's death was imminent. I had already gone to bed, but actually hesitated before getting dressed, wondering if I should put my make-up on before going to see her. Some fears are so deep-seated they defy common sense.

That night I sat by her bed, held her hand, and told her that I had forgiven her. It wasn't exactly an act of bravery, considering that she was comatose at the time. After several hours, the nurse told me I should go on home because Mom's vital signs had improved. I leaned over, kissed her on the forehead, and told her I loved her. This woman who had not responded to anything or anyone in days whispered, "I love you too." God gave each of us a gift that night. She never rallied again and four days later, she was gone.

My reaction to Cholene's call wasn't just based on the fact of her being gay. The load of *junk* I had carried for nearly sixty years affected everything in my life, and it affected my reaction to this as well. It was a bit like moving all the junk away from the entrance to the basement so I could get down there and see about the real issue—why the furnace isn't working. My *furnace* hadn't been working for years.

CHAPTER 5

Let God Sort It Out

I would like to say that this was the end of my questioning, doubting, and agonizing, but it was not. I was quite the hard head. One day at a particularly low point, I called a good friend who is a devoted Christian. She had received "the call" from her daughter about a year before I received mine. She had already traversed some of the difficult roads I was now traveling. She was, and still is, a role model for me. I asked her, "How do you reconcile the scriptures with loving Leigh?" Her answer was, "Well, I can't. So I just love her and let God sort out the rest." It was the best advice I have received on this issue. She has told me some other things along the way that have been invaluable to me. A woman had questioned her for "accepting Leigh's lifestyle." She told this woman, "I don't know how to *not* love my daughter." Someone else asked her where she and her husband "drew the line." This friend was concerned about the logistics of a gay relative and his partner coming to visit. Should she let them share a room? Evelyn's answer was that they didn't draw the line, a position not popular with evangelical Christians. That night she talked to God about it and asked Him where they should draw the line. His very clear response was, *"You don't draw the line. I do."* When Evelyn saw her friend the next week, she shared this with her. Her friend smiled and said that was exactly what God had told her.

My attitude on the subject of homosexuality had been very rigid. I had sat on church pews long enough to form the opinion that there was no wiggle room in this area. Then, when several of my friends' children were "coming out of the closet," I was not seeing *abominations;* I was seeing the faces of kids I loved. I started looking at the scriptures differently. I have been a *rule follower* all my life. I have never had a problem with authority—I never questioned it. Perhaps I should have. I have blindly believed what I was told without thinking for myself or taking it to the Highest Authority. I would virtually put my hands over my ears whenever anyone had an interpretation of the scriptures that didn't jive with what I had been told to believe. But I began noticing that "sin" for Christians tends to be cafeteria-style—we pick and choose what we deem to be sin—and of course that will never be anything that is going on in our own lives. There are many other items listed as sin and abominations that we Christians don't like to think about—strife, envy, greed, all sexual sin, anger, drunkenness, dissensions, slanderers, foul mouthed revilers—and that isn't an exhaustive list.

My mind was wandering one Sunday morning as I looked around the auditorium of our large, non-denominational church. There were people of different sizes, different modes of dress (some "churchy," some casual, some extremely casual), different races, possibly even different political affiliations (although it was basically a *conservative* church). Then I had this thought: *What if everyone in here who is committing any of the sins listed in the Bible were asked to leave the church?* I knew the answer to that one—the church, including the pulpit, would be empty. We rationalize all the other sins as, "I'm only human" or "nobody's perfect" or the more ecclesiastical response, "God isn't finished with me yet." We even regard sexual sin with a wink, a nod, and a shrug of the shoulders. Or, for a lot of us, there is sexual sin in our own pasts that we wouldn't be too willing to share with the congregation. Some of our children chose to live with their partners before marriage. I didn't like it, but I didn't bombard heaven every day, begging that they be delivered as I was now doing on Cholene's behalf; not because I thought *God* considered it the worst sin, but because buried deep in an area of my mind that I refused to acknowledge, *I* did.

Somehow, homosexuality has been singled out as the worst of the worst on the *sin* list. Everyone else is welcomed into church with open, loving arms, but if you happen to be gay, you had better get your act together and cleaned up before you cross the threshold of most churches.

When I surrendered my life to Christ in 1971, it was my understanding that God threw "come as you are" parties. Thank goodness! The friend who told me I could have a personal relationship with Christ recommended a version of the Bible she thought I would enjoy and I set out for the Christian bookstore to buy it, wearing my *uniform* of the day—hot pants and go-go boots. It still makes me laugh when I think of that poor store clerk who waited on me. He looked up, he looked down, he looked everywhere except at me. But—he never made me feel *unclean*. If he had, it would have all been over. I would have turned my back on Jesus and said, "Who needs this?"

When I finally stopped telling God (much later) what He should think and do about this situation and gave Him the opportunity to speak, I was shocked at His reply. It seems that He was much more concerned about my lack of love than He was about Cholene's sexuality!

My friend Edwina continually reminds me of something from Byron Katie's book, *Loving What Is:* "There's my business, there's your business, and there's God's business." This area was definitely God's business— even though I was trying very hard at this point to make it mine.

CHAPTER 6

Iraq

Approximately six months after Cholene's call, life had resumed a sense of normalcy and I stopped being such a "stress tab"—one of Cholene's endearing names for me. Then I got an e-mail from her. I often get an e-mail or a telephone call from Cholene when she is about to do something dangerous that she knows I won't like. Her calls are sometimes from the airport as her flight to some dangerous, hotspot in the world is announced. Then, of course, she doesn't have time to hear of my worries or any flak that could be forthcoming. I have always marveled that she has so much courage. I don't know where she gets it— certainly not from me! Not from her father either. I remember a time when we were married and a mouse ran through the kitchen of his mother's home. He jumped up on a chair and screamed, "Mama!"

I at least credit myself with not keeping her from doing the things she loves to do. I usually don't like it, but I try not to transfer my fears to her. Her e-mail said that she had an "opportunity" to be an embedded reporter if the United

States became involved in the crisis in Iraq. Other options were available to her, but I knew she would choose this one. She joked about having seen war from 70,000 feet (as a U-2 pilot), and now she wanted to see it from 5 feet $4^1/_2$ inches (her height). I was not amused.

Sure enough, she took a leave of absence from United Airlines and went to the Middle East about a month before the start of the Iraq War. She told me that she was representing Talk Radio News Service. I didn't realize it was a specific company. My experience with talk radio was all of a conservative nature, so I was pleased that at least she was going to be reporting for "our side." Have I mentioned that I can be really naïve?

For a while, we were able to communicate through e-mails. Then, about the time the war escalated and she was on the verge of going into Iraq with the Marines' First Tank Battalion, my computer crashed. I panicked! It was my lifeline to her. I took it to a computer repair shop, and they were in no hurry to fix it. In fact, it was in the shop nearly the entire time Cholene was in Iraq. The local radio stations didn't carry her broadcasts, so the owner of Talk Radio News Service, Ellen Ratner, kept me informed by sending me CDs of the broadcasts—usually three-way conversations with Cholene, Ellen and a radio show host. I was enormously grateful to receive them, but it quickly became apparent that this was not a conservative-owned company.

One day during a telephone conversation with Lisa, my son Chip's wife, she asked me what I thought of Ellen. I laughed and said, "She's something else, isn't she? I don't let

James listen to the CDs of her radio shows." On the conservative scale, my husband rings the bell at the top. Lisa asked me a few more questions and suddenly it became clear. "Lisa, are you telling me that Ellen is Cholene's partner?"

There was a brief period of silence, and then, "Oh my God. Chip's going to kill me. I thought you knew." I calmed Lisa down and told her Chip wouldn't know what she had done if she didn't tell him, because I certainly wasn't going to. But, unlike her deceptive mother-in-law, she spilled her guts to him. I heard much later that he told her there was no problem because Cholene had e-mailed me about it right before going into Iraq. (See reference to computer crash above.)

Things were spinning out of control—*my* control, anyway. I felt utterly helpless. In hindsight, I can see where it was God's plan. I once heard a tape by Corrie ten Boom; she said that at one time she had such a grip on something that God had to pry her fingers off, one by one. It was a graphic mental image at the time, and one that I knew I could apply to my own obsession with being in control—another little character flaw of mine.

I resumed banging on Heaven's door. It was one thing to know that Cholene was gay but celibate; it was quite another to know she had a partner. I was obsessed with the thought that God would stop protecting her. Cholene has been in many dangerous situations throughout her life and I am convinced that if it were not for the grace and protection of God, she would not have lived through some of them. Because of the unspoken "don't ask, don't tell" agreement between us, I had no idea until I edited her book, *Through the Eye of the Storm,* over three years after the initial phone call, that Cholene had been aware of her sexuality from the time she was a child. What was I thinking? God knew all about her—He created her. It's not as though He looked down one day and said, "Whoa! I didn't see that one coming!"

I am ashamed of my lack of faith throughout the three months that she was in the Middle East. Whenever possible, I was glued to Fox News Channel. I had a perverse need to know everything that was happening in Iraq, regardless of how much it frightened me. A good friend, one of the few people who knew about Cholene, told me one day that she felt she had something from God for me. There are times when God lets one of us mere mortals deliver a message for Him. Unfortunately, this has been misused by people who just want to straighten someone out, and it has nothing to do with God at all. I have occasionally felt that I had a message for someone, but by the time I finally got up the nerve to give it, along with all my disclaimers about how this may or may not be from God, I don't think it has been too effective. Nevertheless, I have a lot of confidence in Mary, and this was the message: *"Shari thinks I have stopped protecting Cholene because of her homosexuality. I have not. I will bring her out."* I knew it was from God because it was exactly what I had been thinking and I had voiced that concern to no one but Him. Mary also had a scripture for me. *"A bruised reed He will not break . . ."* Matthew 12:20a (AMP) I don't think "bruised" in this scripture means imperfect or flawed; I think it means wounded—emotionally wounded from blows inflicted by the world that God never intended for any of us to receive.

God had spirited Cholene away to a place totally out of my realm of *protection*—a place where I could depend only upon Him for her safety. By doing this, He forced me to focus on my love for her, not on the stranglehold my belief systems about homosexuality had on me. I remembered all the times God had brought Cholene through dangerous circumstances. I had felt then that He had a plan for her life. Nothing had changed. I knew she was going to be okay.

CHAPTER 7

Return from Iraq

I guess parents have a tendency to think that our children are going to follow in our footsteps regarding political affiliation. When Cholene returned from Iraq, I was enormously relieved and thankful that she had returned home safely, but I was amazed that she sounded like a liberal. I'm not sure which fact was harder to deal with at that time—that she was gay or that she might be a liberal.

We live in Odessa, Texas, twenty miles from former President George W. Bush and Laura Bush's hometown of Midland, Texas. There are some liberals here, but most are conservatives. This area is also considered part of the Bible Belt. I haven't always considered myself a Christian. As I stated in the introduction, my family did not go to church, and I attended whenever friends or neighbors invited me. I went away to a Catholic college after my junior year in high school because my parents thought it would break the fascination I had for the man who would eventually become Cholene's father. It didn't. He was Catholic and I attended the Catholic Church throughout our six-year marriage. It didn't occur to me, nor was it important to me, during my *Heinz 57* religious background that I could have a personal relationship with Jesus Christ until I was twenty-eight years old. It was at that time that I got my second divorce and realized I needed some help—I wasn't doing all that well on my own. As far as politics went, it was not discussed in my parents' home. To this day, I don't know if they were Democrats or Republicans. Personally, I try to avoid politics. Cholene's father was a politician—possibly another reason for my avoidance.

I had felt for some time that our country is deeply divided over politics, religion, and gay issues, but now our family was affected. I blamed Ellen. I was sure that this flaming liberal, gay rights activist had seduced my daughter and poisoned her mind. I said as much to my son Chip and he assured me that this was not the case. In fact, he told me that Cholene was the one who pursued the relationship. I was upset that Cholene was conversing with Chip about Ellen, but not with me. Chip and Cholene are very close—now. When they lived at home, it was quite different. When she was three years old, he gave her a spin in the clothes dryer, and when they were both in junior high, Chip a ninth grader and Cholene a new seventh grader, he told everyone she was adopted. I was delighted that as adults, they had such a great relationship—until now. I was jealous of their relationship that seemed to exclude me. I wanted to be the one she confided in, but I hadn't made that easy. I imagine it was difficult for her to be forthcoming about a relationship she knew I didn't approve of. She probably also resented the fact that I asked others about her instead of going to her with my questions.

A few months later, a friend of Cholene's and ours who lives in New York planned to come to Odessa and she asked Cholene to come with her. She was writing an article about the oil industry, and wanted James to show her around and introduce her to some of the oil company owners in this area. James has worked in the oil industry for over forty years, so he was quite willing to do this. (The fact that Hilary is drop-dead gorgeous was another nice incentive.) When we picked the girls up at the airport, Cholene was quite distant, and it seemed she would rather have been anywhere in the world but in Odessa, Texas. It was uncomfortable. The next morning Hilary and James left and Cholene and I stayed home. We sat at the dining area table and talked—but you have probably heard the expression about not discussing the elephant in the room. I don't remember what I said, but I asked her some questions about Ellen's family. Cholene warmed to the subject and it seemed like safe ground for a start. Then we were talking about Ellen, and it didn't take me long to realize that Ellen was no monster. She was a decent human being with a loving family— but most important, my daughter loved her. The rest of Cholene's visit was delightful. The ice had been broken and we were comfortable with each other again.

I met Ellen the following summer. I went to New York with Edwina and Linda, two friends I grew up with in Española, New Mexico. I needed all the moral support I could get. Even though I had "thawed" somewhat, I wasn't convinced that Ellen was right for Cholene. All I really knew about her was that she had been active in the gay rights movement and that she was a liberal—in my book at that time, two counts against her before I even met her. Cholene lived in New York and Ellen came down from Washington, D.C., for the occasion. We met Ellen for dinner in a private dining room of the Times Square Hilton, a hotel owned at the time by her brother Bruce. Ellen and I were both nervous—it was sort of a "Church Lady meets Gloria Steinem" type of thing. By the end of the evening, I had come to two startling conclusions: One, Ellen was not my enemy. Two, I liked her—a lot.

Over the course of our stay in New York, I learned a great deal about Ellen. Some misconceptions I had about her were harpooned along with some about homosexuality in general. I was under the impression that all homosexuals recruited—that they preyed on young, single people and introduced them to the "lifestyle." This was behind the Boy Scout drama—as in not allowing homosexual men to be scout leaders. It seemed that the whole country got in on this action. (Of course it also played on another misconception, phobia, lie, rumor, or whatever you might want to call it, and that is that the words "gay" and "pedophile" are synonymous.) Ellen dispelled my recruitment notion when she told us of a young woman who played around with thoughts that she might be gay and Ellen told her adamantly that she was not—that it was a hard life and not something for wannabes. I was surprised (and immensely pleased) to discover that Ellen was a kind, compassionate, and caring person. One of the things that had puzzled me about their relationship was that Cholene is one of the kindest people I know; I couldn't understand how she could care for someone who wasn't. Is Ellen opinionated, outspoken, feisty, and argumentative? Oh, yes—but she also respects the opinions of others. And like Cholene, she is more interested in promoting others than in promoting herself.

When I returned home from New York, I had a lot of thinking to do. Paradigm shifts don't come easily. I was of the "my mind is made up, don't confuse me with facts" ilk. I was prepared to dislike Ellen, and I was comfortable with that feeling. But I left New York feeling genuine love for her—what the heck was I going to do with that?

CHAPTER 8

The Invitation

One Sunday morning toward the end of September 2004, I was sitting in the non-denominational church that we had been attending for about four years, waiting for the service to start. I was reading the church bulletin and noticed that a Bible study for women was scheduled to begin soon. It was Beth Moore's, *Believing God.* I love her studies. She is down-to-earth, honest about her own faults and failures, hilariously funny, and I can apply her teaching directly to my life. I had not attended one in a long time because of my work schedule, but this particular announcement seemed to be *highlighted* for me. I signed up that morning.

The study lasted over a ten-week period and consisted of our working in a workbook at home, then discussing our answers and comments in small groups before watching a DVD of Beth Moore presenting the topic for the next week. At the end of the first DVD, Beth made the statement that we would face something during the coming week that would challenge our faith as it has never been challenged before. I didn't give it much credence. I should have.

That week I received an e-mail from Cholene (again with the e-mails!) stating that on the fourth of December she and Ellen were planning to be married in Cambridge, Massachusetts, at Harvard University's Appleton Chapel. This possibility had been in the back of my mind from the time all the controversy began about same-sex marriage, and I had been concerned about it. I couldn't listen to a Christian radio program or the news without hearing about gay marriage, or drive the streets without seeing bumper stickers taking a stand against it. I played the "what if?" game a lot. However, there is a huge difference between possibility and reality. When I received Cholene's e-mail, I realized that I was still hoping and praying that she would somehow "come out" of homosexuality. Because I loved Ellen and didn't want her to be hurt, *my* plan was that she would "come out" as well. (You've probably heard the one about how to make God laugh—tell Him your plans.)

The wedding invitation had a sense of finality to it. This wasn't going to go away. I then tried to imagine what it would be like to watch my daughter marry another woman. My mind just could not accept it, and I couldn't see myself going to the wedding. I was planning to have a knee replacement soon, so I immediately thought this would be my reason to stay home. Yet, I was so thankful that Cholene had invited us. I knew the courage it must have taken to risk having the happiest day of her life ruined by parents who might not be all that excited about it. She had to have been struggling with the decision. This was confirmed later when I tricked my son Chip into telling me how long he and his wife, Lisa had known about the wedding plans and it had been at least a month before she told us. Although I couldn't imagine attending the wedding, I would have been hurt had Cholene not invited us. It was a no-win situation for her.

I immediately forwarded Cholene's e-mail to a trusted friend, along with my panicked cry for help. Edwina should be named, She Who Has Level Head On Shoulders and Keeps Dingbat Friend From Going Off Deep End. She fired a response back saying essentially, "If you don't get your act together and support her in this, you will regret it for the rest of your life and your relationship with Cholene will never be the same." I took note. Regardless of the circumstances, Cholene was my daughter. I loved her so much it hurt, and I decided that I wanted to share this important day in her life.

Two hours later, after I had time to digest all of this and have an attitude adjustment, James came home from work. After I told him about it, he said, "Don't make any travel arrangements for me." I was furious with him. Now mind you, I had just had the same reaction two hours previously, but I was expecting him to be at the same point I was at that moment. To my credit, I remained calm and said, "You do what you think you need to do, but I'm going." Knowing James as I do, I knew he would mull it over and come around, but it was going to take more than two hours. After a couple of days, I gave him a copy of Edwina's e-mail to read. Later he told me that she was right; he had worked for too many years to gain Cholene's respect to lose it over this. "Besides, I love her and think of her as my own daughter."

At the beginning of the Bible study the next week the facilitator, our pastor's wife, asked, "Did anyone have their faith challenged this week?" *Oh, yeah!* She then had us divide into small groups of two or three so we could discuss it more intimately. There were several women participating in the study and, oddly enough, I wasn't sitting close to anyone I knew—which was a good thing. A woman from another church and a woman I had seen at church, but didn't know well, *partnered* with me and we went to a remote spot in the room. I guess I looked like I was about to bolt, because they zeroed in on me, and asked if I wanted to talk about anything. Then it all came tumbling out, complete with sobbing. I don't know what I expected, but there was no shock, no revulsion, no sympathy—there was only love and a positive, *you can do this; God is with you* attitude, and of course they prayed for me. The woman from the other church had to drop the study, but Kala and I are friends to this day.

Throughout the ensuing weeks of the study, I learned many things about my relationship with God—such as, I believed *in* Him, but I didn't *believe* Him—I didn't trust Him. I have had trust issues all my life, but until then I did not realize that I didn't trust God. He adjusted my attitude little by little as different challenges surfaced. One week Ellen sent material for a dress in case I wanted to have something made from it to wear to the wedding. It would go with what the two of them were wearing. At first, I thought she was afraid I would wear something unsuitable, but then I realized it was my own insecurity speaking—Ellen wouldn't do that. She was being genuinely helpful. It was a beautiful satin material, but not a color that I can wear near my face. I half-heartedly looked at patterns to have something made. I then decided to buy a top of a different color and have a skirt made from the material she had sent. Again, I dragged myself through stores, looking for something that might work. Also, my knee was giving me so much trouble that I couldn't wear high heels, so whatever I selected would depend on footwear. During this time I worked a thirty-minute drive from home, so it was good prayer-time; also, God often had little "chats" with me at this time, probably because He could get my undivided attention. I was obsessing (again) over what to wear for the wedding, and I heard very clearly: *If Cholene were marrying a man, wild horses couldn't keep you out of the stores until you found the perfect thing to wear.* He was right. My quandary ended. A friend and I went shopping and I found the perfect top. I then found a dressmaker and told her what I had in mind for a long skirt. Since the wedding was to be at night, I felt I could wear a long, formal skirt. That would solve the shoe problem. It was getting dangerously close to wedding time, but she assured me that she could get it done for me.

In the meantime, even though Ellen didn't know what I would be wearing, she sent me a beautiful little designer's purse that couldn't have completed my ensemble more perfectly. We serve a God who cares about fashion when it comes to some of His very, very vain children. In other words, He cares about what concerns us.

Something interesting about the shoes—I selected clothes for the trip around two pair of shoes I could still wear. One was a pair of ankle boots to wear with pants and the other a pair of dress shoes with a short heel for the wedding. There were many events planned, including Cholene's fortieth birthday party, so it was important that I look good. (See reference to "very, very vain" above.) The week we were to go to Boston, I was at work holding the door open for a man delivering a tank of oxygen that was strapped to a dolly, and he ran over my little toe! Other than some crummy-looking tennis shoes, the only shoes I could get on that foot were the ones I had selected for the trip. God is good.

I don't mean to make it sound as if this was all a light-hearted lark. It was not. There were a lot of tears, a lot of pain, and a lot of "I can't do this. It is too hard." Several years ago, someone from the Christian community wrote about the physical aspect of a male homosexual relationship in graphic detail. I don't know why he felt compelled to do that, unless he felt that if someone wasn't already convinced that it was an "abomination," that would certainly do the trick. It put images in my mind that I could do without. Whenever my mind drifted to the physical part of Cholene and Ellen's relationship, I immediately thought about something else. But then, I don't sit around thinking about our other children's sex lives either. (Nor do they want to think about ours. As my son Jason would say, "Eeuuww!) I kept trying to visualize the wedding in comparison to the traditional weddings I had seen, but it was too painful.

I felt like such a hypocrite. I wasn't advocating gay marriage, but I was upset with the side (the side I used to be on) that was blasting it. It had become personal. I have discovered that God teaches me the most important lessons when the issue becomes personal. It's easy to jump on the same bandwagon my peers are riding, but when it involves those whom I love, I have to question the validity of it. I can't blindly follow the pack. I have to decide for myself, with God's help, where I am going to stand and what I am going to believe.

During another drive to work shortly before the end of the Bible study, I was praying—no, make that whining—about the wedding. I was taking the Loop 250 exit off Highway 191 in Midland when God spoke to me so clearly that I thought He was sitting next to me in the car. Since that moment, my thinking has been forever changed. I had asked Him, "What event could a parent possibly be asked to attend that could be more difficult than this?" His response was short. "A funeral."

I told my son Chip about this on the phone later, and he didn't speak for a moment. Then in a quiet voice he said, "That's interesting, Mom, because Cholene has felt that it would be easier on you guys if she were dead, than to know she is gay."

What kind of a message had I given my daughter that would make her think I would rather she be dead than gay? I thought back over the many close calls she had had with death through the years. Was she disappointed that she didn't die? Did she think that would have been easier on me? I knew then that my struggle was over. I didn't understand homosexuality, I didn't understand same-sex marriage, and I didn't understand why my daughter was gay; but I knew Who did, and it was His business, not mine. I let it go.

At the next Bible study, I knew that if the opportunity presented itself it was time for me to *come out from under the bed*. (I have told Cholene that gay children might come out of the closet, but their parents come out from under the bed.) The woman who was facilitating that night opened the microphone for anyone who had something to share. I knew who that "anyone" was, and I knew that God was nudging me out of my chair. My mouth didn't have an ounce of spit in it, my heart was pounding in my chest, and as I stood, I wasn't sure my legs would carry me. You have to understand that I am a speaker. The microphone is my friend, and I (usually) welcome any opportunity to speak. I had looked around the room that night to see who was there. Two women whose husbands work with James were also attending the study and I wasn't sure James would be comfortable with my *outing* him. I didn't see them. Weeks later I discovered that they had been there—I think God hid them because had I known, I wouldn't have had the courage to speak. I don't know if they told their husbands or not, because nothing was ever mentioned to James. I told the group the whole story, including the wedding invitation and God's comment about the funeral. All my fears about how this would be received were unfounded. I felt nothing but love from those women. Some of them told me of their own stories—mostly about gay family members whom they wanted to love but felt they weren't supposed to. One woman had a gay sister-in-law whose father, a minister, had *excommunicated* her from the family. The rest of the family had to sneak around to have a relationship with her. A young woman told me as she looked intensely into my eyes that things would get better. I had the feeling she was trying to send me the message that she was gay. I wanted to pursue this, but it wasn't the time or the place. I didn't see her again. It was a large church with two services on Sunday mornings, so that was not unusual. My speaking up seemed to release others from their secrets also. As for me, I felt like a two-ton burden had been lifted from my shoulders. I was free—free from the worry, free from the need to control, free from the secrets, free from the guilt, free from the feeling that it was all up to me. I finally relinquished it all into much more capable hands than mine.

CHAPTER 9

The Wedding

Now that I wasn't obsessing over the wedding itself, I started worrying about embarrassing Cholene. Ellen's family is definitely on a different socio-economic plane than we are. I was afraid we would be a *country comes to the city* type of thing. Her family is Jewish, ours is Christian. Although I consider Jews to be God's chosen people and, because of Jesus, consider myself an adopted Jew, they may not see it that way. Her family members, for the most part, are liberal Democrats; we are conservative Republicans. I wrote of my concerns to a close friend and she e-mailed me the following mantra that I was to repeat often. "Shari Johnson is a class act." In fact, our first night in Cambridge when James and I were in the hotel elevator on our way downstairs to Cholene's fortieth birthday party, I was saying over and over in my mind, "Shari Johnson is a class act. Shari Johnson is a class act." Thank you, C.c.

If you ever have an opportunity to attend one of Ellen Ratner's "events," don't miss it. She has the gift of hospitality like no one I have ever known. It was an incredible weekend—from facials, to manicures/pedicures, to make-up for the wedding by the professional artists at Fox News, to a tour of Cambridge on a double-decker bus. Ellen has some marvelous, loyal friends who rally for her and manage to help her pull off the most amazing feats. Cholene's birthday party had a Mexican theme complete with Mexican food and a mariachi band—neither of which could have been easy to find in Boston, Massachusetts! Every minute detail had been planned for the guests so we didn't have to worry about anything, including transportation.

It is said that opposites attract, and I guess that can be true of all relationships. Cholene and Ellen are as different as any two people you will ever find. Both of them are kind, compassionate, helpful, philanthropic, and willing to promote others over themselves, but that's where the similarities end. If Cholene had planned the wedding, it would have been much different. Where Ellen is superfluous in everything she does, Cholene is a minimalist. She would have met the guests at the hotel in her running clothes and said she was going to take a short run and would be back in about three hours. If we got hungry, there would be some nice bagels and grapefruit in our rooms. She would go on to say there were probably some interesting things to see in the area, the wedding would be Saturday night, it was within walking distance, and it would do us some good to walk because we probably needed the exercise.

My only disappointment that weekend was that our whole family was not enjoying this together. Other than Chip and his family and Valerie, her half-sister on her father's side, Cholene had not invited the other kids in our family to the wedding. I knew that this had hurt some of them—and it hurt me. Valerie was two years old when Cholene's dad and I married. She, Chip, and Cholene have always been close, but Chip and Cholene were not raised with her—they were raised in our home with Laron, Phillip, Jeff and Jason. I had finally worked through my jealousy of their relationship with Valerie—my feeling that they loved her and the Espinoza side of the family more than they loved me and *my* side of the family. Chip and Cholene were able to convince me that there was enough love to go around for everyone; that love wasn't mutually exclusive. I didn't ask Cholene why she didn't invite them, but I supposed it was because she felt it would put them on the spot. For one thing, it would have been very expensive for them right at Christmastime, but they might have made the trip anyway to support her. They wouldn't have wanted her to think they didn't "approve." When I tried to explain this to some of them, they said they would have liked to have been given the opportunity to decide for themselves. It's never easy to know what to do.

James and Ellen hit it off beautifully. She immediately told him that she had never known a real, live, card-carrying NRA member before. He retorted that when she came to visit us in Odessa, he would remove the guns from the rack in the back window of his truck so she wouldn't feel uncomfortable. (There is no gun rack in the back window of his truck.) Ellen is an inveterate animal lover. She stopped eating chicken after seeing *March of the Penguins* and didn't even get rid of Pavo, her beloved turkey, after he broke her nose while she was hugging him. (I have always said that it isn't a good idea to hug a turkey.) James loved regaling her with his hunting stories, just to watch her squirm. I was so relieved that they hit it off. Of course, Ellen telling James when she met him that he was quite a hunk and if she weren't gay she could really go for him probably had something to do with his instantaneous affection for her.

Cholene's birthday party was wonderful. Everyone mingled, got acquainted and had a great time. Keep in mind that this was December 2004, right after George W. Bush's re-election. One of my worries about that weekend was that there might be a lot of political conflict. It would be safe to say that most of the guests that weekend were Democrats. Had John Kerry won the election, I don't know that I would have been as gracious as they were. We saw each other as people—not as liberals and conservatives. I had to smile when I saw conservative James, a history buff, sitting at a table, deep in conversation with a lesbian couple about historical sites in and around Boston. Everyone accepted us, befriended us, and made us feel welcome. I had to wonder if the same would be true if any of these people were among a group of Christian conservatives. I would like to think that they would be treated as well as we were—but I rather doubt it. During the party, Ellen asked James, Chip, and her two brothers, Bruce and Michael, to say something about Cholene. The tributes were poignant and special. When Ellen came to our table later, I asked her why she only asked men to say something. She said, "You can have your turn tomorrow night." *Oh, (expletive)!*

Edwina and Linda, the friends who went to New York with me when I first met Ellen, had been *encouraging* me (their word—mine would have been *nagging*) to give a toast at the wedding reception. I had come a long way, but I hadn't come *that* far. There was absolutely no way I was going to give a toast. The "tomorrow night" Ellen spoke of was the wedding reception. I could hear Edwina and Linda laughing all the way from New Mexico.

When we went up to our room, I lay awake listening to my grandsons party in the room next door, and begged God to get me off the hook. Instead, about two o'clock in the morning He gave me the words for the toast. I stopped worrying about it and went to sleep.

It was a Jewish ceremony performed by a rabbi, and quite interesting to both James and me. Not being the traditional wedding ceremony we were accustomed to made it easier for us. Chip and Lisa's sons, Chase, Chance, and Chandler, were ushers and their three-year-old daughter, Charli, was the flower girl. Chip is an ordained minister, and he took part in the ceremony by reading scriptures.

I thought of the time when he was a ninth grader and president of the student body in his junior high school in Hobbs, New Mexico. The student council was planning a prom and Chip was in charge. It was held off the school premises, so it was an enormous undertaking for a fourteen-year-old. James and I stepped in to help. This would not have been a big deal, except that we belonged to a church denomination that didn't believe in dancing. One Sunday after church a woman approached me, quite upset. She was raising her grandson and she said, "My grandson wants to go to that dance the school is having and I told him he couldn't go. Then he tells me that you and your husband are running it!" I said, "This 'no dancing' rule is man-made, and one day this church is going to decide that it's okay to dance. Chip needed our help and I refuse to lose my son over this." I was proud of Chip for thinking his relationship with his sister was more important than what anyone else would have to say about his participation in a gay wedding.

After the ceremony, because I couldn't navigate the stairs well with my painful knee and toe, James and I were the only ones who rode down in the elevator. I said, "Well, we made it." He held me, and we both cried for a brief moment. They weren't tears of sadness, but rather a sort of relief that we had come so far and all was well—our time of crying was over and we felt genuine joy.

The reception was a lovely sit-down dinner in a private dining room. There were toasts throughout the course of the evening and I wasn't sure if Ellen even remembered our conversation from the night before. I now know that, except for her keys, she forgets NOTHING! Chip introduced me and I was perfectly calm. Although I enjoy speaking, I am always nervous. However, I wasn't the one in control here. I knew that whatever came out of my mouth was God's business. The amazing thing is that I can still remember what I said. I sometimes don't remember a talk the day after I have given it, and I always speak from notes. I was definitely *winging* it, if you'll pardon the pun. I will just hit the highlights here:

"There once was an evil king who was bored with his life, so he decided to throw a party. He invited liberals and conservatives, lefties and righties, Christians and Jews, gay people and straight people. His plan was to sit back and enjoy the fun while his guests tried to kill one another. But his evil plan was thwarted when, instead of concentrating on their differences, his guests focused on the things they had in common.

"My son Chip says something very profound—confusing, but profound. He says we tend to love those who love those whom we love. You love our Cholene, so we love you. We love your Ellen, so you have to love us."

I said some other things and then something came to mind that hadn't been there the night before.

"A young woman from our church told me one day that she was dating a man of mixed race, and asked me what I thought of that. I told her that it didn't matter, but that she should ask God to show her his heart. We have seen some beautiful hearts this weekend. Thank you, Cholene and Ellen, for bringing us together with all of our differences."

Something I learned that weekend in Cambridge, Massachusetts—not only can I believe in God, but I can trust Him. Several people said that they couldn't describe it, but there was such a "spiritual" feeling to everything that weekend. Yep—He shows up when we least expect Him!

CHAPTER 10

Problems vs. Predicaments

Through the years I have had the pleasure of hearing some of my son Chip's sermons—either in person or on tape. I love having his sermons on tape because I can listen to them again and again. Each time I do, I hear something new. Recently I was replaying a sermon he preached in 2001 in which he explained the difference between a problem and a predicament. He cited something from the book *Management of the Absurd* by Richard Farson, M.D. that really got my attention. Most *problems* people think they have are not problems at all—they are predicaments. And when someone treats a predicament as a problem by trying to *solve* it, it only gets worse. Chip went on to say a problem is something that happens *to* us; something goes wrong, such as a bad experience, an illness, an accident, or a mistake. But a predicament is a result of our own value system. Prior to this, I thought "predicament" was a lightweight problem—like arriving at a writer's conference without luggage and attending the opening banquet in jeans.

He gave consumer debt as an example of a predicament.

Some conditions we might value that would get us into this predicament are instant gratification, convenience, "I deserve it," or "Buying things makes me feel good about myself," image (as in keeping up with the Joneses), or the ever selfless "I want to help the economy." Most people treat debt as a problem and work at getting the balance to zero. Research shows that two of three who succeed in doing this go right back into debt. They didn't work on their value system. Predicaments cannot be solved; they can only be coped with. Yes, I coped with wearing my jeans to the banquet, but anyone who knows me can tell you that it challenged my value system of dressing appropriately big-time! However, it was not a problem, it was not a matter of life and death—it was a predicament.

Bingo! I realized that when Cholene told me she was gay, I saw it as a problem—one of gargantuan proportions. And, of course, I set out to solve it. Now, because of Chip's sermon, I see that it had not been a problem, but rather, a predicament.

I started thinking about my own value system. What did I value that made it so hard for me to accept Cholene's homosexuality? I then realized that, in my case at least, the words "values" and "appearances" were interchangeable.

I have already mentioned that physical appearance was extremely important in our household as I was growing up, but other values were important also. There were definite "guidelines" to how things should or should not be done. My mother didn't work outside our home, and very few of my friends' mothers did. It was expected that women took care of the home as in cleaning, cooking, washing, ironing, and childcare. After I grew up and married I always worked outside the home, but I maintained the old value system and nearly worked myself to death in the process. I guess I got some sort of *payoff* in showing people what an amazing superwoman I was. My mother always fixed a big breakfast on Sundays because that was the only day my dad was home from work—but my family didn't go to church. After James and I married I would rush around on Sundays, pushing a houseful of kids to get dressed and to church on time, but also insisted that everyone sit down to a large breakfast because that was how it was done and what would people think of me if I didn't fix waffles or pancakes with all the trimmings for breakfast on Sunday? It got pretty dicey. I can hardly recall a Sunday when someone, usually me, wasn't fighting, screaming, or pouting on the way to church. Of course, when we got there I had my Sunday smile plastered on my face—and should have had a big red "H" for hypocrite plastered on my chest. Finally, James convinced me that no one would die if we had sweet rolls for breakfast on Sunday—his way of helping out. I had created the *predicament* of chaotic Sundays because I wouldn't turn loose of a *value* that didn't even make sense. Cholene's sexuality threatened my longtime value system of appearances.

Another value of mine, although it took me a long time to recognize it, was one common among parents—bragging rights. Oh, how we love to brag on our amazing children—and Cholene had always given me plenty to brag about. After listening to Chip's tape I remembered an incident that happened when I was a dental hygienist. I had a patient who would tell me about her gifted daughter in great detail at every six-month appointment. One day she was unusually quiet, so I asked her how Cindy was doing. I received a terse reply that she was fine, so I dropped it and we talked about other things. Out of the blue, about halfway through the appointment she blurted out, "She got a tattoo and had her nose pierced." Had she not been close to tears, I would have laughed. Having Jason for a son had stretched my value system somewhat, but Beverly was new at this. Cindy had never done anything in her life but make her mother proud. Beverly was definitely not proud of this new Cindy. When Cholene told me about her sexuality, it wasn't on the approved list of things parents brag about.

I also looked at some values concerning homosexuality that I acquired through the years. Whether or not a person is Christian, attitudes about gay people abound. I valued marriage between a man and a woman, and anything else was unthinkable. I valued the traditional family. I picked up the values of others—such as pastors and other Christian leaders. My values isolated me and made me think that I couldn't share my pain over Cholene with anyone because they would judge her. I had seen it happen many times; something happens in a Christian's life and instead of reaching out for help, we feel that we have to go it alone—that we have to have it all together or we won't be "accepted."

By the time I became a Christian I had been divorced twice. James grew up in a denomination that was adamantly opposed to divorce—so much so that divorced men were not permitted to serve on the church board, and certainly not permitted to be pastors. James' divorce was the first in his family. When we married, we attended churches of this same denomination. As hard as I worked in the church to prove that I was as good as those who hadn't been divorced, there was always the feeling that our family was tainted in some way. Although I didn't recognize it at the time, when Cholene told me she was gay the old feeling of unworthiness returned.

I truly thought I knew the mind of God because of the values I had acquired concerning homosexuality. I went to Boston for Cholene's wedding with my values set firmly in place. Perhaps a better term for "values" in this case would be self-righteousness. I had been telling God what the "problem" was for two years. I made Him well aware of what *my* values were, but I never asked about *His*. It soon became apparent that the thing He valued most was love—and He loved all these people who seemed to have such a different value system from mine. Not only that, but He made it crystal clear that I was to embrace this value of His also.

CHAPTER 11

Unconditional Love

I have always struggled with the concept of unconditional love. I find it unfathomable that God could love us enough to give his Son in death for us. Would I be willing to give the life of one of my children for those who plotted the death and destruction of September 11, 2001? No. Had I been the one hanging on the cross, would I have asked my Father to forgive those who were causing me agony, spitting on me, and mocking me? No. Perhaps that's why I have felt the need to "work" for God's love. I have had a hard time believing that He could love me as I am. I suppose I pictured God using some heavenly stun gun if I got out of line. It's also the reason why, except for loving my children, I had not been able to love unconditionally. As long as you thought as I did, fulfilled my expectations, and didn't cross me in any way, I would love you. Otherwise, zzzztttt!

Our trip to Cambridge challenged my thinking. I realized that I hadn't even scratched the surface of who God is. I started to understand the love of God and, in so doing, came to understand the freedom of loving unconditionally. I have told Cholene that her wedding rocked my world—and my world needed to be rocked. I felt genuine love from and for the people I met that weekend. Most of them are as far removed from my world as anyone could get, yet I care about them, want the best for them, and am always eager for news about what is happening in their lives—as if we have been lifelong friends. Prior to that weekend, I would not have thought it possible. However, my new attitude was about to be tested.

Not quite two weeks after the wedding I went to Washington, D.C., to attend the White House Christmas Press Party as Ellen's guest. As a White House correspondent, she can invite one guest to the party, and since she knew I am a fan of George W.'s, she invited me. I was thrilled. I didn't vote for George Bush just because he was a Republican—I voted for him because I felt that he had integrity, was intelligent, sincere, honest, kind, compassionate, warm, friendly, loved God, and was someone I would be comfortable with inviting into my home. That hasn't changed. These things are important to me. It is my own *value* system.

Cholene was flying a trip, so I didn't get to see her until after the White House party, but it gave me time to get to know Ellen better. And the better I knew her, the more I liked her. I also discovered that Ellen has many conservative friends—something that really surprised me.

The night of the White House party, I felt like Cinderella. It was magical. The Christmas decorations were everything they are touted to be and more. I had to keep checking to make sure my mouth was closed as I took it all in. Soon after we went into the White House, people were escorted to the line waiting to be presented to the president and the first lady. I was mentally practicing what I would say to him. An opportunity like this just doesn't present itself every day. Ellen told me there would be an introduction, a brief conversation, and then our picture would be taken with President Bush and Laura. Things had to move along at a pretty fast pace because there was quite a long line of people. Ellen had already informed me that it was protocol for the news correspondent to stand next to the president and for the guest to stand next to the first lady, but since I was such a fan, she graciously let me stand next to the president. Ellen and I were on the ends, and the president and Laura stood between us. He and Laura were everything I expected them to be—warm, welcoming, gracious, and down-to-earth. After I was introduced as being from Odessa, Texas, I told the president that we love him in West Texas. He replied that he was grateful for the great start he got there. At least I think that's what he said. It's hard to listen when your mind is telling you that this can't really be happening. The picture was taken and then I heard a familiar voice from the other side of Laura say, "Mr. President, I just married her daughter." *Yep, this can't really be happening.* Everything started moving in slow motion from that point. Laura looked around at me with a sweet, but quizzical look on her face; President Bush looked at me with an expression of, "Did I just hear what I thought I heard?" and I, not to be deterred from my speech, with who knows what kind of look on my face, said in a weak little voice, "We're praying for you, Mr. President." As we were leaving the area, there was a lighthearted repartee going on between Ellen and the president—she said that gay people are about making families, not destroying them, he asked if she voted for him, she answered that she was a Democrat, he shook his finger at her and said that she was a journalist, and then it was over. When we got into the hallway, Ellen, not at all concerned that she had just detonated a grenade, asked me what he said to me. I told her that I didn't know. And at that moment, I didn't. I was in shock.

When I have told this story, some have asked me if I wanted to kill Ellen. Even though I believe that I am the first parent in history to have been "outed" to the President of the United States, once I recovered from the shock, I wasn't upset with her at all. I only saw the humor in it. *You've come a long way, baby!*

I learned some interesting things about liberals, conservatives, and the news media while I was in Washington. It seems that while the rest of us are in a rage about what the liberals (or conservatives) are doing, the very ones who have whipped us into this frenzy are friends and they socialize after the various news programs are over. I'm talking about fraternization among liberals and conservatives here. Therefore, it is my belief that it all boils down to ratings and money.

Those in the news media aren't the only ones who keep things agitated. I have listened to different ones in Christian programming who will rant and rave for an entire program, then at the end say, "Go in love." *Excuse me? I am ready to wipe these scumbags you've been talking about off the face of the earth and you are telling me to "go in love"? I don't think so!*

I was so out of control during the 2004 presidential election that I had to stop watching and listening to the news and Christian programing. Forwarded e-mails were also problematic. Most of the ones I received were of a conservative nature, but a few brave liberals in my life sent me some as well. Yet all of them—conservative and liberal alike—contained the same theme. Hate. Whenever I saw what the message entailed, I deleted it. I still do. As a Christian, I am commanded to love. Believe me when I say that I felt no love for the liberals during this campaign. I knew that my attitude wasn't pleasing God, and since I wasn't able to keep things in perspective I had to back off completely. I still avoid controversy on both sides because I just can't handle it. I get too emotionally involved and it makes it nearly impossible for me to love unconditionally. But it has helped to know that we are, in a sense, being duped by both sides. Some might say this is business, so get used to it. It's hard to take it lightly when it is splitting up families and relationships. It isn't just a matter of Democrats and Republicans— it includes religion, gay issues, racial issues, family values, patriotism, wars, education, the workplace, and any other topic that could divide America. There have been times when I have feared another civil war in our country.

Right before the 2004 election, a liberal friend and I were joking about canceling each other's vote. We remain friends because we don't talk politics. She said, "You know, when it comes right down to it, we all want the same things. We want our children to be safe and have nice things, we want good jobs and enough money so we don't have to struggle, and we want to be healthy and happy."

I thought about what she said when we took four of our grandchildren to Six Flags Over Texas in Dallas. As I was people-watching, I thought:

> *Everyone here is on common ground. We are all tired, hot, and sweaty; we are spending a ridiculous amount of money; parents are short-tempered with each other and the kids are acting like brats—but we are all determined to have a good time and to do something nice for our children or grandchildren. No one gives a rip about who is liberal and who is conservative.*

While writing this book, I acquired a new dog. You're thinking, "Big deal." Please bear with me while I tell you the story. First, I have not been an animal lover. I tolerated them (barely). However, my husband is an animal lover and has a beloved, but spoiled, Beagle-mix named Sissy. After several dog-less years, I acquiesced when I saw James watch Animal Planet with tears in his eyes. We rescued Sissy from a terrible fate at the animal control center. (Whenever she acts up, I drive her by the place and remind her of what she owes us. It's quite effective.) After returning from a trip, I picked Sissy up from the boarding kennel. The lady there told me about Sissy's new friend, Mr. Henry, a Chihuahua-mix she was holding in her arms. He had been rescued from starvation and abuse, and she asked me if I knew anyone who would like to have him. About that time, Henry reached out, touched me lightly with his paw, and licked my hand. I told her I would check around. When I got home, I couldn't seem to get Henry off my mind. He was a funny looking little thing, so I wasn't smitten because he was so adorable. He had a cute Chihuahua face, but he had long legs and a body that reminded me of that repulsive little character in the *Lord of the Rings* movies that keeps saying, "precious." I told James about him, but we agreed that we didn't need the added expense of boarding another dog when we travel. A week later, I decided to call the kennel and if 1) Henry was still available and 2) the kennel would give us a good rate for boarding him, I would go get him. It was yes on both counts. Because he knows how I feel about pets, James was shocked when he came home that night and discovered that we had an addition to the family. Henry rarely leaves my side and was curled up next to my feet while I was writing this book. A friend felt that Henry was a little guardian angel of sorts, sent by God to help me through this process. One morning I was reading my Bible (with Henry at my feet, of course) when all of a sudden I knew exactly why I have him. He is everything in a dog I've never wanted. He's a small, hyper, ankle-biting yapper with a machismo complex who refuses to be totally *potty-trained*—and on top of that, he's a Chihuahua—not one of my favorite breeds. Yet I love this little dog as I have never loved another animal, no matter what irritating stunt he pulls. I agree partially with my friend; I believe that Henry was sent by God—but the purpose was to continue teaching me unconditional love. Well, He had a donkey speak to Balaam, so why not? (Read this wonderful Biblical story in Numbers 22:21–34.) Of course, Henry hasn't spoken to me . . . yet.

One last thing on unconditional love: Apparently I am a slow learner, because when I met my granddaughter's fiancé for the first time all I could see were tattoos. They seemed to be everywhere—at least over the parts that I could see. (I've got to tell you that I have never understood tattoos or body piercing, but let's just add those to a long list of things I don't understand. I don't understand electricity either, but I haven't stopped using it.) The problem was I didn't look beyond the tattoos to Chris' heart. I now know that he is a kind, caring, loving young man who loves my granddaughter, treats her well, and is a great father to our great-grand-daughters. I couldn't ask for a better grandson-in-law. Chris loves God, but he avoids church because of people like me who would only see tattoos walking in the door. Please forgive me, Chris. I'm determined to get this unconditional love thing right.

CHAPTER 12

Love Your Neighbor

There are eleven scriptures referring to loving your neighbor in the Bible. The first one is Leviticus 19:18 when God was giving the rules to Moses, and the others are found in the New Testament. I will quote Jesus from Matthew 22:37–39 when He was asked by a Pharisee (they were always trying to trip Him up) which was the greatest commandment. *"'Love the Lord your God with all your heart and with all your soul and with all your mind.' This is the first and greatest commandment. And the second is like it. 'Love your neighbor as yourself.' All the Law and the Prophets hang on these two commandments."*

In Luke 10:25–29, there is an interesting account of a lawyer asking Jesus what he needed to do to inherit eternal life. Jesus, as He often did, turned the question back to him and asked what was written in the law and how did he read it? The lawyer replied, *"'Love the Lord your God with all your heart and with all your soul and with all your strength and with all your mind;' and 'Love your neighbor as yourself.'"* Jesus told him that he had answered correctly and if he did this, he would live. Of course, being a lawyer, the man had to take this a step further. He asked him, *"And who is my neighbor?"* Now I've got to tell you that had I been asking the question it would have gone like this: "Excuse me, but could you clarify what you mean by neighbor, because I don't want to love anyone I don't have to."

This is where Jesus tells the parable of the Good Samaritan in Luke 10:30–37. You might know the story, but it won't hurt you to read it again.

> *"A man was going down from Jerusalem to Jericho, when he fell into the hands of robbers. They stripped him of his clothes, beat him and went away, leaving him half dead. A priest happened to be going down the same road, and when he saw the man, he passed by on the other side. So too, a Levite, when he came to the place and saw him, passed by on the other side. But a Samaritan, as he traveled, came where the man was; and when he saw him, he took pity on him. He went to him and bandaged his wounds, pouring on oil and wine. Then he put the man on his own donkey, took him to an inn and took care of him. The next day he took out two silver coins and gave them to the innkeeper. 'Look after him,' he said, 'and when I return, I will reimburse you for any expense you may have.'*
>
> *"Which of these three do you think was a neighbor to the man who fell into the hands of robbers?"*
>
> *The expert in the law replied, "The one who had mercy on him."*
>
> *Jesus told him, "Go and do likewise."*

I believe that today, in the twenty-first century, God is still telling us to go and do likewise. The gay people I know have a handle on this Good Samaritan thing. One example is very close to home. Cholene and Ellen went to Mississippi after Hurricane Katrina to see how they could help. You can read about the experience in depth in Cholene's book, *Through the Eye of the Storm*. And, since all proceeds from the sale of the book go toward a community center in Delisle, Mississippi, you will be helping with that worthwhile project as well. (I know—a shameless plug.) It couldn't have been an easy decision for them to make for at least one very obvious reason. In her book, Cholene tells of voicing her concern to Ellen about two gay women going to the heart of the Bible Belt in the reddest of red states to camp out with two churches [Mount Zion and St. Paul's United Methodist]. Ellen assured her that it would be fine. "We're the gay version of the movie, *Guess Who's Coming to Dinner*."

I have watched Cholene and Ellen give generously and tirelessly of their money, their time, and their energy—sometimes to the detriment of their health. Because I am so close to this project, I have been able to observe what happens after a disaster in terms of "Love your neighbor as yourself." There are those like Cholene and Ellen who throw caution to the wind and know that something has to be done, so they do it. There are those who get out their checkbooks and give generously; there are those who pray legitimately for the people affected by the disaster, but there are also those who pray to see if God wants them to go help, and sure enough, He doesn't. There are others concerned about WIFM—what's in it for me? The possibility of furthering a career or a photo op might get these people to the area. There are those (mainly politicians) who blame someone else for the disaster, and then there are those who sit back, shake their heads, and say that someone ought to be doing something. And so it is that few of us ever act on our obligation to love our neighbors as ourselves.

While looking at the various scriptures relating to loving your neighbor, I ran across a passage I don't remember ever reading. However, I always tried to skim over any references to loving people, so that's no surprise. I guess I thought if I was a good girl and did my best to do everything else commanded of me (after all, I didn't murder or steal), I would be given a pass on the thing about love. Paul wrote in Galatians 5:14–15, *"The entire law is summed up in a single command: 'Love your neighbor as yourself.' If you keep on biting and devouring each other, watch out or you will be destroyed by each other."* Isn't that what is happening to us?

I am reminded of the pharmaceutical commercials on television—after telling us that their drug is the answer to all of our problems, a nearly inaudible voice speaking at warp speed gives us a long list of warnings about taking the drug. God doesn't follow up his scriptures on loving each other with, *"If your neighbor does not look like you, think like you, believe like you or act like you, do NOT love your neighbor."*

Can you imagine how many laws could be eliminated if we loved our neighbors as ourselves? I'm not only talking about laws concerning murder and stealing, but what about OSHA, labor laws, integration laws, and so forth? We have to have rules and regulations because we won't do what is right, and then we gripe and complain because the government is telling us how to live our lives. If we lived our lives the way they were supposed to be lived, the government would have no reason to step in.

I would be remiss to write about love without including what love is, as stated in 1 Corinthians 13:4–7 *"Love is patient, love is kind. It does not envy, it does not boast, it is not proud. It is not rude, it is not self-seeking, it is not easily angered, it keeps no record of wrongs. Love does not delight in evil but rejoices with the truth. It always protects, always trusts, always hopes, always perseveres."* Any questions?

I received a forwarded e-mail of a story with pictures of a 650-pound baby hippo and a giant, male, century-old tortoise. It seems that Owen, the hippo, was rescued on the coast of Kenya, Africa, after a tsunami hit that region. He has adopted the tortoise as his mother, and the tortoise seems to be fine with that. One of the captions reads, "This is a real story that shows that our differences don't matter much when we need the comfort of another. We could all learn a lesson from these two creatures of God. 'Look beyond the differences and find a way to walk the path together.'"

One of my favorite authors is Jan Karon. Father Tim, an Episcopal priest, is the main character in her Mitford series of books. He has taught me more about the love of God; what it means to be a Christian, and how I can live a Christ-like life than any other non-fiction, how-to book I've read, except for the Bible. He often prays "the prayer that never fails: Thy will be done." Had I prayed that prayer when I first received the call from Cholene, I could have saved myself a lot of angst. Instead, I was praying more along the lines of, "My will be done."

As a Christian, I feel that we have somehow lost sight of our commission to love God, to love our neighbors and to spread the gospel of Jesus Christ and His message of love. Instead, we focus on our rights. Hardly a day goes by that I don't get some e-mail or solicitation call telling me how my rights as a Christian have been violated. (And incidentally, I have yet to find anything in the Bible telling us of our *rights* as Christians.) I am as concerned as anyone is about my right to worship, about continuing to live in a free country, and about the principles America was founded upon. But the message we are sending out isn't one of love. Therefore, the message we are getting back isn't one of love either.

An amazing little book, *The Power Within*, compiled by Clara Endicott Sears over 100 years ago from the writings of thirteen authors of that day has recently been republished by Changing Lives Press. It is divided into daily "thoughts." The following is the thought for November 3, written by Katherine H. Newcomb: "People there are who accept the teachings of Jesus Christ to 'love thy neighbor as thy self,' 'to take no thought for tomorrow,' 'to return evil with good'; yet these same people do not love their neighbor, they *do* take many anxious thoughts for the morrow, and they *don't* return evil with good. They separate their lives from their religious belief; they profess faith in God, and live in fear."

My point? There truly is *"nothing new under the sun."* (Ecclesiastes 1:9)

I am corresponding through e-mail with a woman who

wrote Cholene after reading *Through the Eye of the Storm*. She is divorced and the mother of two grown children. She *came out* as a gay person at the age of fifty-five. I grieve with her as she tries to find center between two worlds. In her initial e-mail to Cholene she wrote:

> *". . . What did impact me beyond all else was that I now was viewed so differently by others of faith. I was raised Baptist, converted to Catholicism when I married, and after my divorce, attended the Methodist church . . . Now that I have said aloud those three words "I am gay," my Christianity has all but been dismissed. My morals, my ethics, my doing what is right (and often not easy), was erased by society. The conservative right tells me I am an abomination to the very teaching that has been the fiber of what gave me the inner compass I possess. . . . For the last three years, I have been unable to reconcile this. On an intellectual level, I can discern it. On a spiritual level, I am lost. I stopped attending church. I stopped reading my Bible. I stopped singing the hymns I know so well. I know that I have drifted far from my anchor-hold and not sure if I can ever go back."*

After receiving a copy of her e-mail from Cholene, I wrote her and received this response:

> *". . . I have experienced the secular gay community—and its own flavor of discrimination. I sometimes think, or would like to hope, that the secular Gay disdain for Christians and faith issues from a deep hurt. I can never join in with those discussions when they arise. There is an element to my discoveries of being Gay that I cannot reconcile with.*

91

Morality is morality irrespective of sexual orientation. That comes from being raised to follow a Christian lifestyle, which should not be antithetical to being Gay. . . . At times, I feel that I no longer belong in either the straight or the Gay world. Perhaps there should BE no delineation. I live a very simple lifestyle and try to focus on what is real and true in life. I am the person I always was, but sexual orientation is not the only aspect of who I am. It seems, however, that is the focus. I struggle with this and find that I retreat and self-impose isolation at times.

"*I want you to know that I do not count you or anyone else as people who have* hurt *me. We all have our own accountability for keeping one's own faith. I know God still talks to me even though I pretend I'm not listening. Even in His own humorous way, He speaks loudly. After sending Cholene the e-mail telling of my spiritual crossroads and feeling far from my faith, I found that God had a message for me. As I drove to work the* very *next day, I passed a church near my home. There on the church marquee, in BIG bold lettering, 'Feel far from God? Who moved?'*

"*In essence, I am responsible for my relationship with God. I am not blaming anyone for the chasm I feel that I now stand upon. The precipitous falling away from what I know to be solid ground is my choosing. What I do place upon others is the denial of Christian fellowship. Where is the substance of a great meal shared alone, having been turned away at the family table, having no other hands to join in celebration or sorrow?*

"*I recently had a conversation with another professional and was told, '. . . you know there are churches that will accept your lifestyle . . .and . . . you don't have to tell anyone you're gay.' Her interpretation of religious 'don't ask, don't tell.'*

"I have a great friend in western New York. She is working on her master's in pastoral counseling, is a spiritual director in the Catholic Church she attends, and offers me unconditional love and friendship. She shared her belief that all should be ministered to in the church family. There are no 'special' masses for 'those others.' I frequently ask her to tell God hello for me. She always responds, 'He already hears you.' This is Christianity in practice."

Several years ago there was a popular Christian craze—WWJD (what would Jesus do?). I call it a craze because the marketing end of it got out of hand, as happens with these types of things. Yet it was a wonderful question—one that each Christian should ask themselves before acting on anything. I think if we asked this question before spouting our opinions of homosexuality and how we are to treat those who are gay, the words coming from our mouths would be quite different. Mohandas Gandhi's quote bears repeating here: "I like your Christ, I do not like your Christians. Your Christians are so unlike your Christ."

My husband's uncle, Homer Goodwin, was a Godly man who served most of his life as a missionary in Ghana, Africa, and as a pastor of several churches in Texas. He understood the WWJD concept very well. A man spoke at his funeral who had been an associate pastor of Uncle Homer's in one of the churches in Texas. This was the man's first position as an ordained minister, and perhaps he was a bit over-zealous at the time. He went to Uncle Homer one day, up in arms over a man who wanted to join the choir, but he smoked. He felt that they just couldn't have it! Uncle Homer very calmly told him that this young man's parents had been praying for him for a long time, and that he was brand new to the faith. He said, "We may be making a mistake by letting him participate in the choir. Or, it may be a mistake to keep him from being in the choir. Either way, a mistake will be made. So, since we don't know which way it will go, let's err on the side of grace." I wish there were more Uncle Homers in the world.

Someone near and dear to my heart gave me another beautiful example of love. While I was editing Ellen's book, *Ready, Set, Talk,* a great book full of useful information about using talk radio, talk television, and talk Internet for your particular agenda, organization, or cause (and yes, another shameless plug), she came to Odessa for a few days so we could work on it. James waited in front of the airport while I went inside to get her. When we got outside, standing next to the curb with people coming and going, James hugged her and said with tears in his eyes, "Welcome, daughter." I had to turn away or there would have been a *sob fest*. I knew it was genuine because of his emotion; I knew how far he had come to be able to say it from his heart; I knew he had put all past prejudices, opinions, and teachings aside, and loved her with abandon, as God wanted him to love her. He wasn't "tolerating" her or "accepting" her for *what* she is—he was "embracing" her for *who* she is. I have never loved James more than I did at that moment.

CHAPTER 13

Love Your Enemies

"You have heard that it was said, 'Love your neighbor and hate your enemy.' But I tell you: Love your enemies and pray for those who persecute you."

—Matthew 5:43

Say what? I have just barely passed "Love your neighbor 101" and now Jesus is telling me that I have to love my enemies too? As they would say here in West Texas, "He's stopped preachin' and gone to meddlin'." He goes on to say that if you love only those who love you, big deal! (Paraphrase mine.)

Several years ago, I read something about Abraham Lincoln that I have never forgotten. It seems that a reporter asked the president his opinion of a certain political leader. Lincoln replied that he thought he was a fine man. The reporter then went on to tell President Lincoln how this man had vilified him and the odious things he had said about him. "Now what do you think of him?" he asked. Again, Lincoln replied that he thought he was a fine man.

The reporter was incredulous. "Even after knowing the terrible things he has said about you, you can still say that?" Lincoln answered, "You didn't ask me what he thought of me, you asked me what I thought of him."

We seem to feel justified in tearing down another if they have done the same to us or to our beliefs. I aspire to get to a point in my life where my opinion of someone else has nothing to do with his or her opinion of me. I'm not there yet.

I think the problem most of us have is that we don't know how to identify our enemy. Paul says in Ephesians 6:10–12(AMP), *"Finally, be strong in the Lord and in his mighty power. Put on the full armor of God so that you can take your stand against the devil's schemes. For our struggle is not against flesh and blood, but against the rulers, against the authorities, against the powers of this dark world and against the spiritual forces of evil in the heavenly realms."* Suffice it to say that our enemy isn't wearing skin. Gay people are not your enemy. Christians are not your enemy. Liberals are not your enemy. Conservatives are not your enemy.

The summer of 2005, my friend Edwina met two lovely young women from Lebanon at the University of Malaga in Spain. They were all there for the month of July to continue their studies of the Spanish language. Edwina, Diana, and Mira met when Edwina overheard Diana's frustration in trying to place a call to Lebanon. She needed to call her mother to tell her that they had arrived safely, but couldn't get the international phone card to work. Since Edwina had just figured it out that morning when she called her husband in

New Mexico, she showed her how to use the card. When Diana reached her mother and told her about meeting Edwina and how she had helped her, her mother asked that she put Edwina on the phone. Neither of them understood a word of what the other one was saying, but Edwina could understand the gratitude in her voice. When Diana got back on the phone, her mother told her to stick with Edwina the entire month. This mother knew instinctively that her child would be safe with her.

Not too many years after that, Diana, Mira, and their families were not safe. It was during the horrible conflict that raged between Israel and Lebanon, or more specifically, Hezbollah in Lebanon. As Edwina received e-mails from Diana and Mira telling of the horrors there, it was apparent that there was (and possibly still is) confusion in identifying the enemy—on both sides of the conflict. In truth, the enemy is the one who plants hate in the hearts of men and women.

Most of us face the enemy issue on a more personal level. I met a woman who showed me how a Christian could and should love her *enemy*. It was one of those times in my life when I felt an immediate rapport with another person. A few hours after meeting her, I felt that I had known this woman all my life—and I trusted her with abandon. After superficial information was exchanged, I learned that she had been married for eighteen years, divorced for six, and had three children; a twenty-year-old daughter, a son about to graduate from high school and a son in junior high. A sense of peace and the love of Christ emanated from her.

I met her at the airport in Dallas, along with another woman—a delightful bundle of energy who made me laugh and feel wonderful. She also was full of the love of Christ—it just manifested a bit differently. The three of us were on our way to a writer's conference and we became instant friends. We boarded our flight out of Dallas to our final destination, and when we arrived at our hotel, we went into the coffee shop for some lunch. There was a long bench seat against the wall with one long table and one smaller table in front of it. I misunderstood where I was to sit and sat at the smaller table across from a woman from California who was also attending the conference. She was already finished with her lunch and preparing to leave, but decided to stay and visit with us for a while. I don't know if you have ever been *set up* by God, but this was definitely a setup! We were among the last of the lunch crowd, so we essentially had that part of the room to ourselves. The conversation among the four of us was not idle chitchat—it was deep and profound communication. The woman from California told us that she worked as a church secretary, but was planning to quit because the pastor was so adamantly opposed to homosexuals and anyone else who didn't believe exactly as she did. Bells and whistles were going off in my head and my heart was pounding—a sure sign that God wanted me to speak up and I, of course, didn't want to. When we finished eating, I asked them if they were in a hurry to leave. They weren't. I then told them about Cholene and the book we were planning to write to help other families in our situation. Lana looked at me for a long moment, then she said in a quiet voice, "The reason I am divorced is because my husband left me for a gay relationship." At that moment I thought, *I don't have a clue about what real pain is.* Lana had every reason to be bitter, angry and full of hate for her husband and this man—this *enemy.* Instead, she told us the most amazing story of what God did for her and through her.

Her husband's partner had suffered so much guilt about breaking up her marriage that he had tried to commit suicide. He was in the hospital, and Lana knew that she had to go see him. She was told later that there were other visitors in his room at the time, but she didn't see them. She had tunnel vision and could only see Wayne. She walked over, stood at his bedside, and told him she did not blame him for what had happened; that had he not been the one, it would have been someone else. Apparently her husband had struggled with his sexuality all of his life, although she did not know that while they were married. Later she was told that there had been some other people from the gay community in that hospital room. After she left, they said never had they seen a Christian display the kind of love they had witnessed that day. The love of God is a powerful thing.

CHAPTER 14

The Ripple Effect

No man—or woman—is an island. Like it or not, whatever we do in our lives is going to affect others. When someone makes the decision to *come out*, it is a lot like throwing a stone into a pond. The ripples the stone causes far exceed the area where the stone hit the water. Families, friends, co-workers, acquaintances, and others will all feel the "ripple." Some of the people affected are changed for the better, and some are not.

I have heard of instances where co-workers have treated a gay person differently after he or she *came out*, and some friends of longstanding shunned them altogether. Thankfully, this isn't always the case.

One area where it really gets tricky is with children—those of the gay person or their nieces and nephews, and the children of friends. Leigh, the daughter of one of my closest friends, has graciously given me permission to relate a situation that arose in their family. Leigh and her sister, Marie, live in different cities. Marie's daughter, Dawn, is very close to her Aunt Leigh. Marie told her sister about a conversation she had with Dawn when she was getting her ready to go visit her aunt by herself for a week. It seems that Dawn had asked her mom why Aunt Leigh wasn't married, and she explained to her that she was gay. When Dawn asked her what she thought about it she answered, "She's my sister and I love her." Marie added, "Nothing more needed to be said." After Dawn's visit was over and she had gone back home, Leigh wrote the following e-mail to her mother, Evelyn:

Leigh:

"There are a few things that bug me about the whole situation.

1. My response when Marie first told me (of her conversation with Dawn, Leigh's niece).

I asked her what she wanted me to tell Dawn if she asked. It's weird . . . I was potentially going to be asked about my life and I was asking someone else what she wanted me to say . . . about my life. Ya know, it's hard enough to come to terms with yourself, but then you still deal with "How am I going to help others come to terms?" You try to protect people from something that is harmless, at your own expense . . . definitely weird.

2. I wasn't even sure I would tell her if she asked.

Talk about fear! I have some fear about talking to my eleven-year-old niece about who I am, and who I am is pretty cool if I may say so myself. What's there to be afraid of . . . nothing real . . . but a fear nonetheless.

3. Marie's response (and perhaps yours) when Dawn asked what she thought about it.

Marie's response didn't really answer her question. In fact, that response gets a person out of having to answer. I understand that that kind of response says, "It doesn't matter," but I can't help but wonder if it doesn't imply, "I think it's wrong but it doesn't matter because we are related." Dawn is going to love me too, but is she going to wonder if God loves me; does Mom think God loves me; will Aunt Leigh go to Heaven? I don't know what I want y'all to say, but I don't think "she's my sister/daughter and I love her" is sufficient. Dawn didn't ask me anything, but I would bet that she will eventually ask y'all more—especially when she hears negative things. It will bother her and she will seek help on how to deal with it from you.

"Anyway, just some thoughts I have been kicking around. By the way, when I say, 'bugged' I don't mean I am bugged by you or Marie at all. But rather bugged at how the situation causes such a stir/a worry/ concern, etc. I hope you know what I mean."

When I told Leigh the title of this chapter, she wrote this:

"It is a ripple effect, only we (Cholene, Ellen, my partner, and I) are the ripple. I know that I am "rippling" through the water. I put a lot of thought and effort into making my ripple calm and undisruptive on a daily basis. It is a conscious effort. Everyone else just gets "splashed" into consciousness by a ripple from time to time—when a child asks a question, [or attendance at] a wedding, a funeral, a family reunion. But the ripple keeps on going and trying to keep everyone as dry as possible. At least this ripple does. And it's hard."

Leigh copied the above paragraph to her mom, and because Leigh's mother and I are close friends, Evelyn sent me a copy of her response to her daughter.

Evelyn (Leigh's mother):

"I have to tell you that I don't ever think of you as a 'ripple.' Do we not make adjustments for all the people we love? Do we not make an effort to keep from disrupting anyone's life because of our standards/beliefs/idiosyncrasies? (I'm very aware that I'm a bit different and very opinionated.) When someone is coming to dinner and we know they have preferences, do we not plan the menu accordingly? If we plan to go to a movie with friends, do we not take into consideration their likes and dislikes? Your "ripple" is no greater than anyone else's."

Lana, my friend from the writer's conference, told me that when she and her husband told their three children of their impending divorce and his homosexuality, their first question was, "Who is going to keep the dogs?" But the children also expressed concern about what people would say to them. A friend volunteered to pray a hedge of protection around them, meaning that God would protect them from hearing harmful words about their father's homosexuality. For over six years, no one mentioned anything about it to them, even though it was common knowledge in the neighborhood. The children have been very private about the fact that their father is gay and have told only their closest friends. The hardest time for each of them has been when they entered their teenage years, around the age of thirteen or fourteen. Lana said, *"Unfortunately, Craig has not been very understanding. He is part of a very limited community that has little contact with teenagers. He just won't admit that his sexuality is embarrassing to them. Of course, at that age, even breathing is embarrassing to them, and if you just hang on for a few years, you can breathe again without embarrassing anyone. Instead, he gets very defensive, which has not been very successful."*

In our own family, Cholene is very close to her brother Chip's children. They adore their Aunt Cho. When she came out, their ages were fifteen, eleven, nine, and one. My granddaughter Charli was too young to know anything about it, but the boys already had ideas of their own concerning homosexuality. As I have said, Chip is an ordained minister. I was proud of the way Chip and Lisa handled it, and proud of my grandsons. There were family discussions, giving the boys the opportunity to voice their opinions and concerns and to ask questions. The consensus was that they loved their Aunt Cho. Nothing else mattered.

As I have stated, all of the children were in Cholene and Ellen's wedding. I think the problem the boys had with that was the part about wearing a suit. There was an anxious moment, however, when as they were getting dressed for the wedding eleven-year-old Chandler said, "Well, this ought to be interesting." Chip and Lisa exchanged looks and wondered what was coming next. He continued, "I've never been to a Jewish wedding before." Aren't children wonderful? No wonder Jesus wants us to be like them.

Our grandson Justyn, Jason's son, was five years old when Cholene *came out*. Jason decided that he would wait on having "the talk" with him until he was older. One night while they were having dinner Justyn piped up with, "I know what a lesbian is." It got very quiet while Jason tried to decide how best to handle the situation. He told Justyn it was good that he knew that, and they would discuss it after dinner. After they finished eating, Jason took Justyn to the living room, sat next to him on the sofa and said, "Okay son, you said that you know what a lesbian is?" Justyn very proudly said, "Yes. It's someone who crosses the street." Don't you just love a kid who doesn't know the difference between a lesbian and a pedestrian—and it wouldn't matter to him if he did?

Jason had the "real" talk with nine-year-old Justyn when he thought Cholene and Ellen were going to be at a family reunion, and he felt it best to get any questions or opinions aired beforehand. It went something like this:

Jason: Son, do you know what it means to be gay?

Justyn: Yes, I think so.

Jason: Do you know that your Aunt Cholene is gay?

Justyn: (Nods his head.)

Jason: What do you think about gay people?

Justyn: (Shrugging his shoulders with palms up)
         They're just people.

Precisely, dear Justyn, they are just people.

There isn't a generation *gap* between the thinking of my

grandchildren and that of my generation—it's more of a generation *gulf*. After pondering this for some time, I have concluded the following: I was not raised to be an independent thinker. I was told what to think by my parents, my teachers and anyone else in authority. I didn't buck the system. This wasn't common only to my situation; it seemed to be typical for my friends as well. In school, rote and memorization were the methods of learning. Think of opening the top of a student's head and spooning in the information. I received a certificate in Dental Hygiene in 1965 and returned to work toward my bachelor's degree in 1970. In five short years, teaching methods had changed. I remember being surprised by a college biology professor when he said he didn't care if we got the correct result in the lab, he wanted to know how we arrived at our findings. This was antithetical to everything I had been taught. The correct answer or result was always the most important thing.

When our children still lived at home, try as I would to make them little clones of me, they were all fiercely independent. They wouldn't buy into "Because I said so!" or "If I want your opinion, I'll give it to you." It drove me nuts while they were growing up, but today I'm thankful. They were open-minded—not that they fell for anything and everything that came along, but they didn't close their minds about an issue or a person until they had the facts; they didn't just accept popular opinion. Today they are kind, compassionate, forgiving, non-judgmental adults and I see those same attributes in their children. When Cholene told me about her sexuality, I wish I could have shrugged my shoulders and said, as Justyn did, "They're just people." I wish I had been more like Chandler—then my first thought when I got the invitation to Cholene and Ellen's wedding would have been that it should be interesting, considering I had never been to a Jewish wedding before. And my prayer for Justyn and Chandler is that their thinking will never change.

The ripple has touched me in ways I never dreamed possible, and I feel that I am a better person for it. If someone had told me ten years ago that I would be writing a book like this, I would have either laughed or turned and run in the opposite direction as fast as my legs would carry me. Will Rogers said, "Go out on a limb—that's where the fruit is." There is fullness to my life and a wealth of beautiful, new relationships I would have missed had I not been forced out on the limb to discover and embrace people who aren't like me.

While I was in Washington, D.C., for the White House party, Cholene and Ellen told me that I should write a book about our experience from the viewpoint of an evangelical Christian. I thought about it on the flight home and for several days after, but I just didn't see how I could write about it. That was entirely too far out of my comfort zone. I wasn't about to expose my vulnerability to the world. Although I had come a long way through working on my "people-pleasing" tendencies, I didn't want to go out of my way to create enemies either.

One day I told a Christian friend what Cholene and Ellen had said, and she told me that I couldn't write the book yet because my story wasn't finished. I knew what she meant; that Cholene wasn't out of the "lifestyle." There was a time when that was the only happy ending I could see also. I had been telling God how things had to happen in order for this story to come out right. After Boston, I knew that He had matters under control and the only things that should concern me were His amazing love for all of us, and the love he wanted me to have for others. I knew this was the message I wanted to convey, but I didn't have a clue about how to put it in writing.

Soon after this, I had a partial knee replacement and while I was still recuperating, James had emergency foot surgery and a serious staph infection. By the time things were back to normal at our house, I had forgotten about writing the book.

Several months later, I took an online mystery-writing course. We were to pick a topic for our book that we felt passionate about. Eureka! I could write my story as a mystery, say all the things I wanted to say and no one would be upset with me, because it was a work of fiction! I was diligent about all my course assignments; I had a good story line, interesting characters, a dead body—everything necessary for a good mystery. I was so excited. But after the class ended, I found I was running into some creative difficulty. It just wasn't coming together. One morning while I was walking, I asked God to help me with it. He took over the conversation from that point, and this is a summary of what He said: *"You say that you want to help other parents who are in this situation and yet you aren't willing to be honest about your own experience. You are hiding behind fiction, and that isn't going to help anyone."* Ouch!

When I got home from my walk and sat down for my Bible-reading time, I asked God for confirmation of this. (Whenever it is something I *want* to do, I never ask for confirmation.) The scriptures in my reading guide for that day were Matthew 16:24–25(AMP):

> *Then Jesus said to His disciples, "If anyone desires to be my disciple, let him deny himself [disregard, lose sight of, and forget himself and his own interests] and take up his cross and follow Me [cleave steadfastly to Me, conform wholly to My example in living and, if need be, in dying also].*
>
> *"For whoever is bent on saving his [temporal] life [his comfort and security here] shall lose it [eternal life]; and whoever loses his life [his comfort and security here] for My sake shall find it [life everlasting]."*

Again, I said, *Ouch!* I remembered something I wrote Cholene when I wrapped up my part of editing her book, *Through the Eye of the Storm*. I said, "Maybe we can do a book together someday and tell our story." I don't know where that came from, because I had never even thought about it. But I now knew this was what we were supposed to do. I e-mailed Cholene and asked her if she would be willing to co-author a book with me. She said she was game if I was.

CHAPTER 15

My Little Black Book

Through the years, I have been accused by many of keeping a "little black book" where I record every affront, slight, insult, offense, and hurtful word—real or imagined—that has ever been directed at me. There is absolutely no tangible evidence of this. I carry it all around in my head. However, I have acquired a *real* black book, and I have been using it constructively to jot down ideas and points I wanted to include in this book. This chapter consists of the contents of that book.

A Matter of Semantics

There are some *buzzwords* surrounding homosexuality that tend to be inflammatory. I inadvertently have used several of them. Cholene told me one day that when I said "lifestyle," it connoted a choice. This surprised me until I thought about the word in other contexts—the old television show, *Lifestyles of the Rich and Famous,* depicted how the rich and famous *choose* to live. As convinced as I once was that homosexuality was a choice, I am now equally as convinced that it is not. I have seen doors closed to my very intelligent, capable daughter that would have been open to her had she not been open about her sexuality. Jason was right—no one would *choose* this. I compare it with salmon swimming upstream. I really don't think the salmon would choose such a rigorous, difficult, painful life, had they not been programmed to do that.

I thought of an analogy concerning homosexuality as a choice one morning as I was walking:

> *A blue-eyed child is born to a family of brown-eyed people. Parents, siblings, grandparents, aunts, uncles, and cousins as far back as anyone can remember, are all brown-eyed. It is not acceptable to this family for this child to have blue eyes, so he is rejected. He is told that he will not be considered part of the family until he changes his eye color to brown. He tries everything, including brown-tinted contact lenses. That satisfies everyone for a while, because he is conforming, but he can't keep it up because the lenses bother his eyes and aren't a good fit for him. He tries many different pair with the same results. He finally gives up and takes them out. True to their word, the family tells him he must leave—he cannot be a part of their family.*

Once I realized that this was not a choice, it clarified something else I had not been able to understand—a husband or wife leaving their marriage for a same-sex relationship. Typically, the partner who leaves is vilified. People cluck their tongues with disdain—much more so than had the partner left for a heterosexual relationship. I have talked with some of those who have left their spouse, and it comes down to a matter of trying to live a straight life and finally having to admit to themselves and to society who they are—as in the blue-eyed, brown-eyed example. To compound the problem, there are now many other people involved—including, in some cases, children. My question for you is this: Who is at fault—the person who cannot live a lie any longer or a society that puts such restraints on them that they feel forced into living the *straight* life?

I have heard of cases where custodial rights have been awarded to an abusive father rather than to the lesbian mother who would provide a safe, loving home for the children. This is outrageous and insane.

A gay man I met who has become a good friend told me he had been married four times, trying to be straight and please his father.

Other situations I know of involve spouses who have chosen to remain married and live in a loveless marriage rather than face the upheaval and fallout. I was told of a gay man who admitted that he felt no affection for his wife, but chooses to stay in the marriage. How can this possibly be a good thing? I can't imagine being married to someone who has no affection for me. In my opinion, this is a tragic situation for all concerned.

If we believe that homosexuality is *not* a choice, then we have to either believe that God is cruel to have played this terrible trick on people and not the loving God we think He is (and that would be a God I could not serve), or there has been a mistake in interpreting the scriptures. I choose to believe the latter. God has not cleared it all up for me, and He probably never will. He expects obedience from me in doing what He has called me to do—love Him and love others. Period.

Other words that I had to re-think were "accepting" and "tolerant." Cholene explained this so well in an e-mail to a friend of mine who was trying to help someone navigate the complicated and turbulent waters of an evangelical Christian mother and a gay daughter:

> *"In terms of the issue of being gay, one perspective is that oftentimes people think in terms of the straight community as being tolerant or accepting of the gay community or individuals. The very nature of this language serves to make gay people feel less than. But then again, this is not limited to the issue of gay or straight. Take, for example, interracial marriage or any marriage where one family or the other isn't quite happy about it. The parties involved eventually accept it. It all implies an undertone of superiority on the part of those who see themselves as accepting or tolerating. [Concerning a gay person and her family], the issue is one of embracing each other in love—not accepting, dealing with, or tolerating—because we all have blind spots across a variety of issues, and the only way to be able to see the beauty of this world is to open our hearts to others—whether they are like us or not."*

I thought I was doing so well by *accepting* Cholene, until I read this e-mail. She was so right. I was placing myself in a position of superiority, although it was not my intention to do so.

Cut Us Some Slack

In my defense (and the defense of others from my generation), we grew up in a different world. For us, the word "gay" meant happy. I will never forget laughing with my friend Carolyn when she told me of an incident that took place at a party she attended. This was probably around 1968. She was sitting alone at a table when a woman approached her and asked if she was gay. Carolyn said, "Oh yes! I'm having a wonderful time."

In high school, if you wore green on Thursdays you were a "queer." We didn't have a clue about what a "queer" was, but we sure were careful not to wear green on Thursdays. And of course having a "coming out party" had a whole different connotation back then!

Our parents didn't share things with us—it was more of a "children are to be seen and not heard and especially not told" world at that time. I remember asking my dad when I was a kid if he had voted for Stevenson or Eisenhower, and you would have thought I had asked him how many times a week he and my mother had sex. He was furious with me and told me it was none of my business and I was never to ask anyone such a personal question again. There was an air of secrecy in our homes. No wonder we are so screwed up!

I was discussing this with a friend recently and she related the following incident.

"I called my son Rick and told him, 'We had a sad visit

from the Baileys. They had some bad news about Megan —she's come out of the closet and announced that she is gay.' While I thought I was being very broad-minded and accepting of the news, my heart ached for them because they had to 'come out' also, and it was very hard for them. Rick responded with, 'Mom, that's not bad news. I thought you were going to say she'd been in an accident or something worse!' I realized that I must have subconsciously thought it was bad news. I was very shocked with my own interpretation. We are a product of the environment in which we are raised, and my exposure to the real world was much smaller than Rick's—so naturally we would make different assumptions about the degree of bad, good, or neutral associated with a subject like homosexuality."

Even though my generation has a certain sense of innocence (or naiveté, if you will), is there something wrong with *not* assuming that every sharp, unmarried woman over thirty is a lesbian and every good looking, unmarried male hairdresser is gay?

Another thing—to you readers who are gay and you have been hurt, disappointed, or angry with the reaction of your loved ones when you *came out* to them, keep in mind how long it took you to come to terms with it. In Cholene's case, it is my understanding that she struggled with it for over thirty years before she could. As I said before, paradigm shifts aren't easy. Years of teaching, thought patterns, and opinions don't usually change in the length of a phone call, or even for months afterward. It is a process.

Seeing the Other Side of the Coin

I usually try to "walk a mile in someone else's shoes," but I was obstinate about the gay issue. I just could not see any other side but mine. Again, some things were brought to my attention. When I was discussing the gay marriage issue with a friend, she told me that a friend of hers, a gay man, told her that it was time for those in the gay community to be accountable to their relationships—that marriage would help to keep some from walking out and going from relationship to relationship. I had never seen it from that side. I never realized that one of my same arguments for heterosexual couples not living together applied to the gay community as well.

A gay woman I know said that she and her partner would like to have the option of being married, but at this point, both cringed at the prospect of all the "awkwardness" it would bring.

Until I saw the movie, *Under the Tuscan Sun,* I did not understand the depth of feeling same-sex partners have for one another. It was a good thing I was watching it on television and alone, because I lost it when one of the characters, an artificially inseminated, pregnant woman, was in gut-wrenching pain over her partner's leaving her. The partner decided she wasn't ready for motherhood after all. It was portrayed so well that I could feel her pain—I then understood the depth of love Cholene felt for Ellen. It is no different from heterosexual love. I have been told by various gay people that they don't understand an attraction for the opposite sex any more than heterosexuals can understand the same-sex attraction.

The movie *As Good As It Gets* with Jack Nicholson and Helen Hunt illustrated the fact that not all gay men are the same—just as not all heterosexuals are the same. I know it seems like a cliché, but people tend to believe what they hear. We Christians get upset when we are generalized as boring, not very bright, bigoted, and hypocritical. Yet that is the perception that many have of us. Gays are often defined by their sexuality; they are characterized as sexual perverts who want to bring as many people into their "lifestyle" as possible. The stereotypes for both groups are wrong.

The only way we are going to be able to love one another as we are commanded to do, is to get to know one another one-on-one. That goes for gays, straights, liberals, conservatives, those of different races, different religions, and anyone else who doesn't think or look like we do. I was able to make my 180-degree turn-around only after I met and got to know personally those I had avoided. As Henry David Thoreau said, "It is never too late to give up our prejudices."

Pointing the Finger

We are so afraid that someone is going to get by with something and that God isn't going to punish some *sinner* that we just *know* needs to be punished. My son Chip gave an excellent example of this in one of his sermons. He said that most of us who drive have, at one time or another, broken traffic laws—and were always relieved if we weren't caught. Yet when someone does the very thing we have been guilty of and passes us when we are going the speed limit or commits some other infraction of the law, we start looking around for a cop, hoping that driver will get his just punishment. And aren't we delighted if we get the opportunity to see him pulled over on the side of the road, looking contrite while a policeman is writing a ticket!

I was listening to a radio interview several years ago when "Sex Respect," a Christian-based abstinence program for youth, was popular. The guest on the show was the founder of that program. She said that the abstinence message was being taken into the public schools, but without the Christian emphasis. When the phone lines were opened, the first caller was an irate man who said that under no circumstances should the Christian message be watered down. The guest explained it was the only way to get the message of abstinence to the kids in school and asked if he did not think it important that those kids hear it. His reply was, "Let them go to hell!" The host and the guest were practically speechless in the face of such bigotry and hate. No, I definitely did not want this man representing Christianity or me.

I was behind a car one day that still bore a popular bumper sticker prior to the gay marriage vote in Texas. It said, "Adam and Eve, not Adam and Steve." Immediately, a song I have heard in churches several times through the years came to mind. Let me *sing* a verse for you: *"For they will know we are Christians by our love, by our love—they will know that we are Christians by our love."* Unfortunately, we seem to be known more by our obnoxious bumper stickers. I would like to see this quote by Deborah Orin on a bumper sticker: "The worst biases are the ones you don't know you have."

One last example of idiocy masquerading as Christianity is something I saw on the Internet when I was seeking copyright information for this book. I Googled "Amplified Bible" and one of the entries read, "The Amplified Bible . . . is straight out of the pits of hell." I rest my case.

The Entertainment Industry

I've said it before and I'll say it again. It's all about the bottom line—money. I used to feel that Hollywood and the entertainment industry in general were cramming acceptance of homosexuality down our throats. I would groan when yet another TV series or movie was *pushing* that agenda. I never watched these programs or movies, so I wouldn't be able to tell you if that were, in fact, the purpose or not. Yet when I went to New York City with Edwina and Linda, I saw something else. Ellen treated us to some Broadway plays, and one of them was *The Producers.* I was appalled at the play's portrayal of homosexual men. It seemed to confirm the stereotype that so many have of gay men. The gay men I know are intelligent, caring, accomplished, successful, loving human beings—not a bunch of buffoons flitting around in tight pants. I could not understand why an industry that could do so much good would perpetuate this ridiculous stereotype. Granted, my feelings were raw at this point, and as I heard the audience laughing, I felt in a sense that they were laughing at my daughter. So here's the paradox: we have the Christians and conservatives upset because the entertainment world is pushing homosexuality; then there are those of us who are upset because gay people are being misrepresented by the entertainment industry. And the entertainment industry? They are making money—and lots of it!

The High Price of Being "Right"

Sometimes people get some loony ideas in their heads and nothing can convince them that they may be wrong. About twenty-four years ago, there was a teaching circulating among Christian circles that Christmas was a pagan holiday. The people purporting this idea presented historical *facts* backing this allegation and some people became convinced that we shouldn't celebrate Christmas. My thinking is that Christmas is the one time of year when people are usually kind to one another—there are even cease-fires during wars at this time. So what if it isn't the exact day Jesus was born? It is His birth that we are celebrating, not the day. Anyway, a man in our Sunday school class at our church in Denver, Colorado, was convinced that it was wrong. He decided that he and his family were not having the traditional Christmas celebration. No siree! No gifts, no tree, no big dinner, no family gathering, no nothing. His wife took their two young sons and went to Oklahoma to be with her parents so they could celebrate Christmas. I have often wondered how he felt that Christmas as he sat alone in his house.

A variation of this sometimes happens when a gay person comes out to his or her family and a father, a mother, a relative, a friend decides that until that gay person "comes to his senses," there will be no relationship. As Dr. Phil would say, "How's that workin' for ya?"

Prejudice and More Semantics

There are two words I have had a hard time saying: "Mexican" and "lesbian." I grew up in Española, a small town in northern New Mexico where there was a large Hispanic population. Although we didn't know anything about being "politically correct" at that time, the word we used was "Spanish." Regardless of where a person's ancestors came from—Spain, Mexico, or Latin America, we referred to them as being Spanish—similar to the way the term "Hispanic" is used today. Even though the Merriam-Webster Dictionary's definition of "Hispanic" includes those of Mexican descent, there are Mexicans who will argue the point and prefer not to be included in that group. But to call someone a "Mexican" at that time was considered racist and derisive. It was a label, and I could not bring myself to use it.

This got me into trouble when I spent Christmas at a classmate's home in Mexico City my freshman year of college. I kept referring to everyone there as "Spanish." That was tantamount to traveling in Ireland and calling the citizens "English." Their eyes would flash and they would say, adamantly, "We are Mexican!" They are fiercely proud of their country and their heritage—we Americans should take note.

I have been on the receiving end of prejudice from both sides of the street. When I was in high school in Española, New Mexico, if I were running for anything requiring a popular vote, I knew my chances were slim because of my Anglo surname. Anglos were in the minority, and even though the Hispanic kids would not have had anything against me personally, or might not have known me, they would often vote for a Spanish surname. I just accepted this as a fact of life. I certainly saw the same situation among adult Anglos, ostracizing those whom they didn't even know based on their Spanish surnames. Cholene's dad was Spanish. His ancestors actually did come from Spain. Because Española was settled by the Spaniards, this is the case with many of the people who live there. After we married, I experienced another type of prejudice. When I was a student at the University of New Mexico, if I called about an apartment for rent and gave my name as Shari Espinoza, there would be no apartments available. I finally caught on to what was happening, and started showing up at the same places I had just called. Amazingly enough there would be an opening. I guess my Irish genes opened the doors for me. I didn't rent from any of those people.

On a lighter note, to point out just how ridiculous prejudice can be, there was a time in my early twenties when my hair was blonde (guess I had spent too much time in the sun). I was working for a dentist in Española and one of our patients was a distinguished, older man who had no use for me whatsoever. He treated me so rudely that I dreaded seeing his name on my schedule. One day when he had an appointment, I happened to have borrowed a dark, short wig of my mother's to wear, just for kicks. (These were the days of wigs, falls, and various hairpieces—ancestors of the modern-day hair extensions.) His appointment went great —he could not have been nicer to me and I was relieved that he had finally come around. I wasn't in the treatment room when Dr. Redman went in to check his teeth and look at his x-rays, but after dismissing the patient he came into the lab to tell me what had happened—although he had a hard time getting it out, he was so *amused*. It seems that my patient told him, "I'm sure glad you got rid of that blonde who was working here. I liked this brunette much better."

As much as I abhor racial prejudice, I was guilty of prejudice of a different nature, and it is equally unfair. We tend to disparage anyone who is different than we are. Although I wasn't a *gay basher,* I didn't have anything positive to say either. I am ashamed to say that I have laughed at others' jokes and comments about gay people. Ellen Degeneres is a wonderfully talented comedienne and I was a big fan of hers—until she *came out* and I got caught up in the Ellen "Degenerate" nonsense. Here was a woman I had admired and one of the few celebrities I would like to know personally—yet when I learned of her homosexuality, I was ready to discredit her. I am now in the position of knowing what it feels like to experience that kind of unfairness. As talented, intelligent, and deeply spiritual as Cholene is, there are still doors closed to her because she is gay.

I have heard the word "lesbian" used derisively, as in "lesbo" and other obnoxious renderings. The delivery of the word is also often irritating to me. It is not just *said*, it's *spat*. For this reason, it is very hard to refer to my daughter as a lesbian, even though there should be nothing defaming about the word. However, words aren't the problem; the attitudes behind the words are the problem. All the *political correctness* in the world isn't going to change anyone's attitude; that will happen one person at a time, one heart at a time.

Retaliation

When Cholene was flying for Emirates Airlines, on one of her flights to Africa she visited Cape Coast Castle in Ghana, West Africa, the place where the first slaves were kept under deplorable conditions before being shipped to America and elsewhere. She heard the story of two men who had been consistently brutalized. They *snapped* and attacked the guards who did this to them. When I read her e-mail, I received some insight and understanding into something that had been a mystery to me. Sometimes when I tell someone about my changed heart and what God has done for me concerning the topic of homosexuality, I invariably get, "Well what about Act Up, and people who march in those obnoxious parades, and if they don't want us thinking they are perverts why do they act like that?" This is said with the accompanying body language of backing up a step and folding their arms in front of them. I didn't have an answer until I read Cholene's e-mail about these slaves. Regardless of whether the persecution is racial, religious, political, or any issue where *they* are different from *us*, when people are continually mistreated, degraded, and hated, the potential for retaliation is present. I see this in the Christian community. You would think that there were a Bill of Rights in the Bible—there isn't. In fact, I have read nothing about our rights as Christians. Rather, there are scriptures about turning the other cheek; love your enemies; when someone wants your cloak, give him your coat as well; and the really tough one—you *will* be persecuted. These are NOT popular verses.

We Christians shake our heads in wonder over Judas' betrayal of Jesus Christ, yet it was a result of his disappointment in Jesus—that He didn't come as Judas and some others imagined and kick the Roman's butts, so he must not have been the Messiah. Judas didn't want a love message, he wanted blood. Are Christians today that much different? Many don't want to hear a "love message" for gay people, liberals, or anyone who thinks differently than they do. They want God to zap 'em, and they are convinced that God is on their side. I know this because, although it shames me to say this, that was my thinking at one time.

In 2006, while reading a little devotional book that I had received at church on Easter, a piece by Max Lucado stood out. It was about Jesus meeting the two men on their way to Emmaus after His crucifixion. They didn't recognize

Him and were surprised that this man hadn't heard about the crucifixion of Jesus. One of them said, "We had hoped that he was the one who was going to redeem Israel." Max wrote that Jesus must have been a bit chagrined—He had just gone to hell and back to give Heaven to Earth, and these two were worried about the political situation of Israel. Max then said that we aren't that much different. "Our problem is not so much that God doesn't give us what we hope for as it is that we don't know the right thing for which to hope."

Along this line, who are we to decide what is best for another? I thought I knew what would be best for Cholene. I didn't. I, of all people, should have known how badly things can go when we meddle in the lives of another. My parents divorced when I was nine months old—this was 1944 when divorce was not a common occurrence. I didn't know of the existence of my birth father until I was ten years old. My mother remarried when I was three, and my step-father was the only father I knew—and he was a wonderful man. When my mother told me the circumstances of my birth, she also told me that my father had tried to kill me when I was in my crib, that he hated me, and that the evidence of that was apparent from the lack of birthday/ Christmas presents, etc. I guess her purpose was to make me hate him as she did, but somehow the message I received was that I was such a loser even my own father didn't love me. That misconception stuck with me and colored the next fifty-plus years of my life. After she told me about my birth father, my mother allowed me to have a relationship with my paternal grandmother, aunt, and two uncles who lived in Colorado—a fun-loving, Irish family. I never asked questions about my dad, and they didn't mention him.

When I was twenty-four, I took it upon myself to meet my father, my stepmother, two of my three half-sisters, and half-brother who all lived in California. My half sister Annette was in Germany at the time. Her husband was in the military. I was able to take Chip and Cholene with me to share in this monumental event. I didn't feel anything but love from all of them—quite disorienting considering what I had been told. There was not a lot of contact in the years before my dad passed away, and I regret that. I felt torn between wanting a relationship with my birth father and my "other" family, and not wanting to hurt the father who raised me.

I went to California for my dad's funeral, and I was not treated any differently than his other children. My stepmother told me something while I was there that was life-changing for me—she told me that my dad had loved me. She had nothing to gain from telling me that, and in fact could have resented my very existence. I was in my forties at the time and I can't describe the feeling of knowing that my father had loved me. Years later when I heard *the rest of the story*, I discovered that I was a victim of *meddling;* of people in my life thinking that they knew what was best for me. It turns out that my dad's mother made him promise that he would never contact me—that I would be better off if he didn't. This, of course, fed the fire of my mother's story. (Note: It is quite possible that my mother may have been a pathological liar, or at least had her own version of truth—the one that fit her needs and agenda best. I now feel quite certain that she had a narcissistic personality disorder.) My father, stepmother, and half-brother have since passed away, but my sisters Annette, Chereyne, and Karen (in order of birth) and I have a beautiful relationship to this day. They have blessed my life. Karen, sent me an album my father had kept of my baby pictures, with his comments written in his beautiful handwriting with silver ink on the black pages. She found it while preparing the house for sale after my stepmother passed away. She knew what it would mean to me. Bob, Karen's husband, put the pictures on a CD set to the music of the Big Band era. My dad was an orchestra leader and my mom sang for his band—that's how they met. I have never received a more treasured gift. I'm probably the only grandmother on the planet who shows everyone her *own* baby pictures!

When my half-brother Rob was dying of bone cancer, he asked me if I could write to his daughter. They had been estranged for years because of . . . you got it, the meddling of others. I wrote her of my experience and told her that even when people love us and think they are doing the right thing, they can make some wrong decisions. She and Rob were reconciled before he died. As long as there is life, it is never too late to set a wrong right.

You may feel that you know what is best for your son or daughter—do you really? I know of same-sex relationships that are beautiful, and I know of heterosexual relationships that are nightmares, and not safe. I know of children in homes where both parents are of the same sex that are far better off than some I know in more *traditional* homes. Many parents whose children are gay or transgender have no problem with it whatsoever, but they still fear for their child's physical safety, fear that there will be employment repercussions, fear period. And would those fears exist if there weren't those out there (Christians, among others) creating that unsafe environment?

Openly Gay

"Openly gay" is a term that confuses me. It is sometimes used by churches in describing those who are not welcome to worship there. Does it mean that a gay couple cannot *carry on* in church? I would be disturbed by that also. But if that's the case, I would like to see the ushers go to some of the heterosexual couples I've observed in church and ask them to "take it outside," or in more modern vernacular, "Get a room!" I sometimes wonder how far these couples are going to go, right there "in front of God and everybody."

If a church takes the stand that "openly gay" people are not allowed to be a part of their congregation, does it mean that it is okay as long as no one knows about it—sort of the ecclesiastic version of "don't ask, don't tell"? So . . . is lying and deceit more acceptable?

Because of the bias of many people, not just those in churches, gays have had to hide who they are. Cholene hid it for 37 years. It is a horrendous dilemma to be a person of integrity, yet have to lie and deceive others. I worked for a dentist at one time whose philosophy about patient care differed from mine. One of my responsibilities was to *sell* cosmetic dentistry. I felt that patients having poor bone support, who would possibly lose their teeth in five years or so, should be told of that possibility before spending thousands of dollars on a smile that could be quite temporary. The dentist felt that he was giving these patients five years of having the beautiful smile they had always wanted, so it justified the treatment and there was no need to tell the patient. Since I was his employee, I had to do it his way. Honesty and integrity are paramount to me—so much so that I became physically ill while working for this man. I quit my job after five months, and there was an immediate improvement in my health. I feel we have forced gay people into a similar conundrum.

I asked a gay friend what her thoughts were concerning "openly gay," and the following is her response:

"I personally would not view myself living openly gay, but rather living openly. Taoism defines living openly as 'having no exceptions.' For me, coming out so late in life was to balance a great familial and societal risk of non acceptance against one's self respect and integrity. Living openly is living wholly.

"To live openly does not imply that one should draw attention to oneself, which begs the question, how out is out? Some individuals who are Gay are out by degrees. Some are out to family, some only to friends, some to co-workers, and some hide in fear their professional counterparts will 'find them out.' I know of two professional

women who have shared a home and life together for years and still present their relationship to their respective families as being 'roommates.' I believe being closeted fosters self-loathing. Those that are closeted are saying, in essence, there is something wrong *with the way I live, with my choice of partner . . . with me.*

"Those individuals belong to an invisible group of people. They are exiled from the community at large, as well as the Christian community, by choice. By silence, they allow the 'conservative-fundamentalist' to decide for ALL of us what defines 'Christianity' and to whom the Christian community and church belongs. Jesus said ALL who are believers are welcome-and He did not place any exceptions on that invitation.

"There is time for a 'call to arms.' There is a time for unified display and outcry, but there is also a greater time to be a gentle listener and to teach by quiet example. As in the practice of Christianity, there is a time to thank God for all our blessings, a time to pray, a time to show love and compassion for others, and to help those that we see in need. Christians who are Gay should not be denied the fellowship of sharing in these tenets in a church that would not deny them to heterosexual couples.

"I don't have a partner. But if I did, I would like to think I could hold her hand during worship, to embrace her with open love in sharing the sign of Peace, to connect *with her in a shared practice of faith and worship. It astounds me that these actions could EVER be construed as wrong or need to be hidden from sight. But we know nothing is hidden from God and it is HIS house!*

"I will not deny that there is a great risk in being out. But were not the Christians in ancient Rome placed at great risk for standing up and saying 'No Exceptions—I

am a Christian'? I too say, 'No exceptions—I am a Chris-
tian—who happens to be Gay.' Risk means consequences.
If we remain silent, remain hidden, we continue to
remain invisible and uncounted in the Christian commu-
nity. And if we remain silent and in hiding, nothing
changes."

Although I have no statistics on this, I have surmised that
many, perhaps even most gay people think they cannot have
a relationship with God. If you ask those on one side of the
gay issue why this is so they might say it is because homosexuals are convicted of their own sin and know that they
don't deserve a relationship with God. The other side would
possibly say they have been told by Christians and others
that they can't have a relationship with God unless they are
straight. But what does God say?

A marvelous book, *Crisis—40 Stories Revealing the*
Personal, Social, and Religious Pain and Trauma of Growing
Up Gay in America, edited by Mitchell Gold with Mindy
Drucker, is one that should be required reading for every
parent, every teacher, every . . . well, everyone. A young gay
man recommended it to me, and his story happens to be
in it. You will look at the gay issue much differently after
reading this book. Toward the end of the book, Rev. Dr.
H. Stephen Shoemaker, a Southern Baptist minister, writes
a chapter titled, "Homosexuality, the Bible and Us." He
quotes an entire sermon he gave at Myers Park Baptist
Church in Charlotte, North Carolina, on July 15, 2001—

exactly one year before I received Cholene's call. (I wonder, if I had heard his message that day would our story have been written differently.) The chapter is fascinating, but one thing really got my attention. Dr. Shoemaker tells of seeing a pamphlet in a church narthex titled, *What Jesus said about Homosexuality*. When he opened it, he found four blank pieces of paper. The words printed on the back said, "That's right. Nothing."

I have learned through this experience with Cholene that the only opinion that matters is God's. He obviously knows all about His children, so who and what are we protecting—God's reputation or the sensibilities of the congregation? Several years ago when I confessed shaking my fist at Heaven to a Christian friend , she told me that God is a big boy; He can take it. I try to remember that.

Friends: Well-Meaning and Otherwise

I have learned something about being a friend through this process. It's too bad I didn't know before this, or I could have been a much better friend to those going through a crisis in their lives.

We were living in Denver, Colorado, in 1983 when the oil industry took a major hit and my husband lost his job of twenty-one years. We were devastated. When I tearfully told a woman from our church what had happened, she very flippantly said, "Oh, don't worry. God will take care of you." I wanted to deck her! Yes, I knew that God would take care of us, but at that time, I needed someone to cry with me.

When it comes to hearing that you have a gay child, there are friends who will just cry with you. They don't try to make you think that they feel sorry for you; they truly hurt with you. It doesn't matter if they believe the same way you do—they love you and they hurt because you hurt. These were the most comforting to me.

Then there are those who can't figure out why you are so upset, because they don't see anything wrong with it. Some are wise enough to keep their mouths shut about their own opinions, and some aren't. It was much later that I discovered my half-sister Karen, who is considerably younger than I am, didn't understand why I was falling apart as I told her and my other two half-sisters about Cholene, because she saw no problem with it. Fortunately, she was one of the wise ones.

There are also those who, because of their beliefs, convictions, dogma, or whatever you'd like to call it, are going to make sure that you understand *their* position on the subject. They often start *preaching* and will tell you what you need to do to "bring her out of it." Like I haven't already been down that road? Some ask me how I can condone it. It is not my call to condone or condemn. I also get many e-mails that slam homosexuals. I have had to develop a thick shell and not take these personally. I think that sometimes people forward e-mails to everyone in their address book, and they are sent to me unintentionally. Other times I wonder. Regardless, it hurts that people I know and love have this opinion of homosexuals—because that particular demographic includes my daughter. I have to remind myself constantly that not long ago I had the same opinion. Of course, there is always the delete button.

Then there are those who want desperately to understand because they love Cholene and they love me, but they simply can't. They are in the same position I was in, and I can't really help them. Help can only come from God. I read a plaque recently that said, "I don't want the peace that passes all understanding, I want the understanding that brings peace." I don't know that I will ever understand homosexuality, but I know that I have peace. I guess that puts me in the "peace that passes all understanding" camp, and I'm okay with that.

Something else—friends become paranoid about an innocent slip of the tongue. A friend at work had gotten a new haircut and it was quite short. She said, "I wanted it short, but I didn't want to look butch." She followed me to my car after work that day, practically in tears over having said that. I assured her that I hadn't given it another thought, and I hadn't. I have been guilty of disparaging remarks myself, although they are all returning to haunt me now. I remember the first time I heard Ellen say, "He's as gay as a goose." It shocked me and cracked me up at the same time. Perhaps we take ourselves too seriously. If we lived in a perfect world, there would be no slurs, jokes, or putdowns about people who are different from us—but we don't.

The Voting Booth

Even though I avoid politics, I make it a priority to vote. I feel that if I haven't expressed my desires and preferences in the voting booth, I have no right to complain about the outcome. I gather all the information available on candidates and issues beforehand so I can make a responsible decision. But this process was far less complicated for me when I saw the world as *black or white;* when I saw things as either right or wrong—no ifs, ands, buts, or maybes. I usually voted a straight Republican ticket and voted along the conservative side of every issue. I didn't have to know what the other side had to say because they were *wrong.*

My experience with the gay issue has caused me to think for myself, so politically speaking, I would need to classify myself as an Independent. I have stated before that I was not encouraged to think independently as I was growing up, and I maintained that pattern of thinking as an adult. I still get angry with myself for having followed the teachings or ideas of others without question. However, it was a long time before my first thought when I had to make a decision over a controversial subject wasn't *what are people going to think of me?* Old habits die hard, but I'm happy to say that I can now look at the facts, and make rational, rather than emotional decisions and conclusions. Or, perhaps it's just that I don't give a rip about what *people* think anymore. It is a bit like watching the pundits on television after a State of the Union address. The president has delivered a message that we have heard with our own ears, yet the *talking heads* tell us what we heard, what we should think about what we heard, and that what we heard was not what we think we heard. I don't stick around for the post-mortem.

I didn't vote when the issue of same-sex marriage was on the Texas ballot. Some issues are far too complicated and personal to be decided by a popular vote. If I voted *against* gay marriage, I would have felt like a hypocrite because I love Ellen as my daughter-in-law, and I'm happy that Cholene has found someone wonderful with whom she can share her life. Yet it would have been hypocritical to vote *for* gay marriage because I feel this shouldn't be decided by an election—I feel that it is a personal issue, not a political one. There was a time in the United States when interracial marriage was illegal. What were they thinking? I didn't feel at the time of the vote that I was qualified (nor is anyone else) to decide what is legal and what is not when it comes to adult human relationships. However, if it comes up again (and I am sure that it will), I will vote *for*. I didn't realize then the pain a surviving partner experiences by having no legal rights to what he or she and the deceased partner built and accumulated together, not to mention the horror of a funeral without being able to either express their own grief or to have their grief acknowledged. In my opinion, it's a matter of human rights and equality—how can I deny anyone else the same rights that are available to me?

While I am on this soapbox, I'll say that I do not understand how same-sex marriage impacts the lives of others. I have heard the most ridiculous arguments about how gay marriage is going to have an adverse effect on all of us law-abiding heterosexuals—including our insurance policies. Give me a break. My rights are not diminished if others have those same rights.

Something else that mystifies me—the Christian community rages on about sexual sin, which would be sex outside of marriage, yet rage equally about same-sex marriage, forcing a gay couple to "live in sin." And as Cholene told me one time, "Because they think gay people are all about sex, you would think they would be happy to see them get married—everyone knows that people don't have sex after they are married." She cracks me up.

Whenever controversial issues play an important part in elections, emotions run high and people cease to think clearly. Furthermore, regardless of which side the politicians are on, the issue becomes just another way to gain votes. I feel this is what has happened concerning gay marriage.

I have already written of the struggle I had with Cholene and Ellen's wedding. The first time I spoke with the wedding planner, a friend of Ellen's who has become a friend of mine as well, she said, "Cholene and Ellen's relationship has given me hope for finding a good relationship." Because she is divorced and heterosexual, it surprised me that she would say that. I have thought about it a lot since then. I have had two unhappy, failed marriages. My mother and grandmother had six divorces between them. Four of our six children have been divorced at some time. At this point for me, the issue over gay marriage is not about the usual pros and cons. It comes down to whether my daughter and her partner who love each other, are kind to one another, bring out the best in one another, and make a dynamic team should be denied the opportunity to publicly and legally declare their devotion to each other. NO!

Don't Ask, Don't Tell (DADT)

How could I write a book about my gay daughter who attended the Air Force Academy and was the second woman to fly the U-2 spy plane without talking about Don't Ask, Don't Tell? You may have seen Cholene on the *60 Minutes* "Don't Ask, Don't Tell" segment that was aired on December 16, 2007.

These are Cholene's thoughts concerning DADT:

For most of my thirteen years in the military, the policy was not "Don't Ask, Don't Tell"—rather, it was "Just Don't." I had personal experience with the military gay ban that still haunted me. I couldn't undo the injustice that was perpetrated upon my friend and freshman roommate, whom I nicknamed "Pup," but perhaps I could save other Pups from her fate.

Pup and I laughed our way through "BEAST," a play on the acronym BCT—Basic Cadet Training that every entering freshman endures. Thankfully, Pup and I had both graduated from the U.S. Air Force Academy Prep School, so we knew how to play the game and most importantly how to laugh at ourselves. We made it through our freshman year and were "recognized" as true Cadets, a ceremony where we were "pinned" by the upperclassmen with the coveted "Prop and Wings," the same insignia worn by the men and women of the U.S. Army Air Corps.

The following summer was full of intense training in SERE (Survival Evasion Resistance and Escape), but compared to an entire year of freshman military and academic training, it was like a meditative retreat. I had just returned from spending ten days out in the field practicing survival and evasion—running around the Rocky Mountains in the middle of the night with bad guys chasing me, and no food. When I walked into Pup's room, I knew something was horribly wrong by the look on her face. I thought perhaps one of her parents had died.

She said, "I have to leave. I'm getting kicked out." What? I couldn't imagine what must have happened. Pup was a solid student, a great athlete, and loved by everyone. She said, "I have a girlfriend." Someone had turned Pup in for having a relationship with a woman off base and Pup didn't lie about it when asked if it were true. I never saw her again.

Four years later when I was a jet instructor pilot based in Columbus, Mississippi, Pup wrote me a letter to check on me and let me know that she was back in New Hampshire, her home state, and doing okay. I'm ashamed to say I never wrote back. I was afraid of being identified in any way with a "Lesbian." Sounds paranoid as I write; perhaps cowardly is a better description.

I never in a million years thought I'd be making the case for gays to "openly serve" in the military to homes across the country on 60 Minutes, *a news program I had always watched and admired.*

I did not have a relationship with a woman until I was completely out of the service, but for years I had adhered to my own version of "Don't Ask, Don't Tell" to most of my military friends, including the gay ones. You could say that secrecy and fear were ingrained in my psyche.

Despite my reservations, I agreed to do the interview. It was a moment of truth for me because I knew that the policy of Don't Ask Don't Tell kept great kids out of the military and caused so many people to leave at a time when our volunteer forces were critically short.

I had been to Iraq twice by that time and knew the tremendous toll multiple deployments were taking on families and our troops. The majority of those serving expressed their sentiments as, "Don't Ask, Don't Care." We (they) were at war. It has been my experience that war tends to put things in perspective. These tremendously dedicated troops were more concerned with what was real than upholding a law that was passed by men and women who were not living their war. The policy of Don't Ask Don't Tell mandated that gay service members hide and lie about a fundamental part of their being. This requirement to lie weakened the very core of military service—personal integrity. If you cannot believe or trust the person whose life your life depends upon, you cannot survive in combat.

Unit cohesion was also diminished due to Don't Ask, Don't Tell. As with any relationship, secrecy creates barriers. Often, people were "out" despite the policy and there was, just as in Reverend Bauman's Christ Church when he welcomed gay people to the Christ Church family, a collective sigh of relief in the unit.

Most important, however, I wanted Don't Ask, Don't Tell to be overturned because I wanted everyone to have the opportunity to serve this nation. My military service transformed me. It built on Christ's example of service above self. It humbled me, trained me, gave me a true sense of passion, a foundation in integrity and great life-long friendships. If I could open doors for more to serve, then I could suspend my fears of being the "poster child" for DADT.

Almost three years to the day of the 60 Minutes interview, Ellen and I had the privilege to watch from the floor of the U.S. Senate as the law, Don't Ask, Don't Tell, was *overturned. There were two bills for consideration that day, Don't Ask, Don't Tell and the DREAM Act (Development, Relief, and Education for Alien Minors Act). The galley was full. Several military members and Veterans were present, but also there were hundreds of kids wearing their caps and gowns, most of whom had travelled by bus for days to be present for this historic vote.*

The DREAM Act was the first matter of consideration. As I watched the Senators make their case for the affirmative, I choked up. Their story was not so different from those of the service members. They were qualified. They desired to serve this country as educated, tax-paying citizens. They had earned their education. But because of the wrong birth credentials, the door was closed.

The DREAM died. I cried. It looked like Senator Durbin, (D-IL) was crying. The Galley cried. Most of the Senate however, was still milling around talking, joking, strutting. If there had been drinks, it would have looked like a cocktail party.

Then the vote on Don't Ask, Don't Tell was raised. The Galley, including the DREAM kids, sat up straight and listened intently to the speeches. The vote began and the kids moved to the edge of their seats.

And then the words were spoken. Don't Ask Don't Tell was now just a part, an unfortunate part, of our nation's history.

I cried again. This time it wasn't because of DADT, it was the DREAM kids—they were clapping, smiling, and cheering. They had been dealt a life-stopping blow just moments before—the right to serve the nation that had just rejected them. Yet they could cheer and express genuine support over the victory of others who also struggled for equality of opportunity.

My feelings about flying and my military experience are best expressed in this poem by Sydney Jewell:

> **Birds of the air have wings**
>   **And so have I.**
> **On earth with the wings of the world**
>   **I tried to fly.**
>
> **God from the height beholding**
>   **My heart's desire**
> **Lent me the wings of heaven**
>   **To come up higher.**

It was at the U.S. Air Force Academy that I fell in love with flying and developed a deep-seated need and desire to serve others. For many years however, I felt as though I was handicapped in my ability to serve because I am gay. Flying, indeed the sky itself, provided me with a sense of home, of belonging. And while the sky will always be home, *I am now able to serve freely, openly, honestly, and fulfill "My heart's desire,"—to empower others "to come up higher."*

CHAPTER 16

Grace

$\mathcal{E}$verything written in this book boils down to one word—grace. My friend Kim sent me something on Grace vs. Law that explains it better than anything I have ever read or heard before. It was in a sermon given in her church by a visiting pastor from Uganda. Paraphrasing Pastor Cyrus in Kim's words:

> *"Law represents human effort, the result of which is always frustration and anger; flesh does not bring liberty, it always brings bondage. The law stops the love from flowing. Grace, on the other hand, depends on God alone and is completely independent of human effort. The two can never be mixed—and when we try to mix them, the law will stop the flow of love. Grace is not a doctrine, it is a person. It is the person of Jesus Christ. Anyone living under the law and trying to meet the requirements of the law (or impose them on anyone else) will always end up hating himself and those he or she tries to impose the law upon."*

When Cholene is in New York City, she attends Christ Church, pastored by The Reverend Stephen P. Bauman. My son Chip introduced them, and Reverend Bauman has been an important part of Cholene's life and a blessing to all of us. His teachings, love, understanding, and grace epitomize the name of the church. One of the members told Cholene that on a Sunday after Reverend Bauman had announced from the pulpit that gay people would be welcome in their church, there was a collective sigh of relief from the congregation. People look to their pastors and their churches for confirmation that it is okay to love their gay children, friends, co-workers, parents. But far too often the message from the pulpits and Christian leaders is not one of love *or* grace.

Author Alexander McCall Smith writes the *No. 1 Ladies Detective Agency* book series—a favorite of mine. The series setting is Botswana, Africa, and in his book *Blue Shoes and Happiness* the main character, Mma Ramotswe who is the founder of the detective agency, was asked by a white lady at a restaurant if she would take a picture of her and her friend. She thought one of the ladies was Botswanan, but the white lady she assumed was from "America perhaps, some place of neatly cut lawns and air conditioning and shining buildings, someplace where people wanted to love others if only given the chance."

I received a "FAITH MATTERS at Christ Church" e-mail forwarded from Cholene and dated March 19, 2010, in which Rev. Bauman wrote (in part) the following:

"Over lunch with a student from Columbia University I learned she had just experienced what she thought was a very great failure; she had been rejected at all three graduate programs to which she had applied. She said that all her life she had worked hard, gotten good grades, but all this rejection made her wonder if she really had anything worthwhile to offer after all. She was poised on the precipice of despair.

"I once read a story about a boy who went up into the attic and drew a circle with a big F in the middle because he hadn't been doing well in school, and then he hanged himself over the F. His problem was that he couldn't distinguish himself between the grade he was getting and who he was as a person. I shared that with my young friend and told her about a few of my experiences of rejection and failure over the years. And although I'm not usually so adamant in first-time counseling conversations, I told her never, ever to hand over her essential identity to anyone other than the God who loved her beyond her wildest imaginings."

I wish Cholene had had the opportunity to grow up in Christ Church. Yet I am beyond thankful that God Himself let her know of her worth and His love for her. It took a while before she could overcome the damage that had been done and look square into the approving, loving face of God.

Cholene:

Again, I was sitting in church. The daydreaming and counting ceiling tiles lost their ability to pass the time quickly enough, so I began to read the text upon which our religion was based. I was introduced to the concept of unconditional love and that all are equal in the eyes of God. I read about a man named Jesus who gravitated to the "less thans" and put those who thought they were "better than" in their place. I loved this man. He became my hero. But there was still this issue of the "defect" in my life—I liked girls. I wasn't acting on this "defect," but I held that notion "in my heart," and so I felt that until I was healed of this sinful nature, I could not be a fully embraced child of God.

I did the only thing I knew might help. I prayed that God would heal me of being gay. I did the greatest amount of praying on this topic during the summer before the sixth grade. I was shipped off to Bible Camp and I have never felt more alone in my life. I cried at the altar every night—partly out of homesickness and partly out of hopelessness. The counselors thought I was the most spiritual child in the camp. They called me a prayer warrior. I was praying all right, praying that God would get me out of this camp and make me like all the other girls—boy crazy.

God answered my prayers on the first account. My father, who was divorced from my mother when I was almost three years old, lived a few hours from the camp in northern New Mexico. He made a deal with the camp counselors to let me go to lunch with him. He picked me up and took me for my favorite meal—hamburger, fries, and a chocolate milkshake. We talked about the camp. I didn't want to go back. I told him that I hated it and I didn't belong there. He said that feeling alone was normal and it was okay that I didn't belong—that he didn't belong there either. But I had to go back—that was the deal we made. I didn't tell him why I didn't belong. He and I never questioned the other's reasons behind our words; we just accepted them as valid. I went back to camp—and I went back to school for a miserable sixth-grade year.

On the eve of the first day of my seventh-grade year, I announced to my mother, "I'm tired of being a loser. I'm going to work really hard, Mom." To this day, I don't know why I decided to emerge from my hole of under-achievement.

I entered the seventh grade with a new purpose in life; I was going to get straight A's. I loved going to school and doing my homework and I became "college material." But inside I knew I was still a scrubby kid. I knew what it was like to be on the other side of the achievement line. I knew what it was like to be a "defect" and I decided that if I worked hard enough and got good enough grades and made the marching band and went to church four times a week, no one would notice that I was a defect. And especially, I would not have time to think about it. But any-time there was a serious altar call, the kind where you lay your deepest, darkest sins on the altar for God to grant the deliverance that has eluded you, I went back to the trusted prayer, "Please God, don't let me be this way." And the word for "that way" today is "gay."

It amazes me that not one Christian could be a Christian if it weren't for the grace of God—yet we are so unwilling to extend that same grace to others that we deem *unworthy*—and can get downright cranky when God does. The author Phillip Yancy calls it ungrace in his wonderful book, *What's*

So Amazing About Grace? Prior to reading his book, I called it hate. Perhaps ungrace *is* a better term. Once I realized that I had been duped, that the *ungrace* I had been taught did not come from Christ, I was angry—angry at pastors, angry at Christian leaders, angry at myself for being so naïve and gullible, and for letting others do my thinking for me. (Cholene's term for this is "Trained Seal Christianity.") I changed churches—several times. Every time I heard the ungrace message, I was out of there. If not for my husband, I would have stopped going to church altogether. I was furious as I left church every Sunday after hearing a message about God's love and grace that apparently was only for certain people—but definitely not for homosexuals. As people sit smugly in their pews and preach from their pulpits, not wanting any more of God than what they are comfortable to believe of Him, people are hurting, families are broken up, and kids are killing themselves.

At the risk of sounding like Church Lady (the Saturday Night Live character), what Christians don't realize is that Satan is delighted. He has convinced those in the LGBT (Lesbian, Gay, Bisexual, Transgender) community that they can't have a relationship with God, and he is thrilled that the hearts of many Christians are so filled with hate that their relationship with God is damaged and their Christianity (and God's commission to spread the good news of Jesus Christ) is rendered totally ineffective.

I have talked a lot about *hearts* in this book. Not too long ago when I was preparing a presentation for the PFLAG Lubbock group, I was thinking about my toast at

Cholene and Ellen's wedding, and about God showing us some beautiful hearts that weekend. I wasn't praying, but God butted in anyway and let me know that He had shown me *my* heart that weekend also—and it wasn't pretty. I'm thankful that, as I once read on the back cover of one of Max Lucado's books, He loved me too much to leave me the way I was.

Oddly enough, I am now closer to God than I have ever been. I have stopped listening to everyone else and started listening only to Him. (Naturally, I thought I had been listening to Him all along.) Concerning my not wanting to go to church, I feel that God is asking me a question I don't want to hear: *If you keep running, who will tell them about how important it is to love?* I am doing the very thing I have done on the other side of the fence—avoiding those who don't think as I do. And I'll be dipped if He doesn't expect me to love the Christians I am so upset with!

CHAPTER 17

PFLAG

$\mathcal{S}$ome time has elapsed since starting this book, and I am surprised at how my thinking has changed. My first inclination was to *soften* a few things—as in soften my former dogmatic point of view. As I have told Cholene, I am light-years from where I was at that time. Although, just because I feel differently about some things *now,* doesn't mean it wasn't my experience at that time. I said in the very beginning that this book would be honest. Just as I can't change where I was before, I can't finish this book without being truthful about where I am now.

Soon after Cholene and Ellen were married, they told me about PFLAG (Parents, Friends, and Families of Lesbians and Gays). They thought it would help me. It is an international organization that promotes the health and well-being of those who are gay, lesbian, bisexual, transgender and provides support and information to their families and friends. It has over 200,000 members and supporters in the United States. I told them it sounded like a good idea and I would look into it. And I did. Five years later. The thing was, I thought I didn't need it. I had *accepted* Cholene's sexuality, so I was *fine*. The closest chapter of PFLAG I could find was in Lubbock, Texas, a drive of two and one-half hours from Odessa. My job precluded my attending their monthly meetings held on Tuesday evenings. However, I was able to attend their bi-monthly Mothers' meetings scheduled on Sunday afternoons. My one regret is that I didn't follow through when Cholene and Ellen first told me about PFLAG. This wonderful group of mothers of gay children has given me support to cope with the negativity that seems to crop up at every opportunity, education to dispel misinformation that abounds, and the safe environment to celebrate Cholene and Ellen's lives and their love. I soon realized that reluctant acceptance is a far cry from full-out joy!

It's difficult to describe the happiness and relief I feel when I can share anecdotes about Cholene and Ellen and brag on their accomplishments without encountering the all too frequent body language (arms folded across chest, one step back, one or more eyebrows raised), or the polite smile that never makes it to the eyes that are saying, "You poor, deluded woman. You are putting up such a brave front."

Although I felt when I first started attending the Mother's meetings that I had found an oasis in the desert, I was shocked to discover that these Christian women who were kind, loving, compassionate, and intelligent did not believe that homosexuality was a sin. I did, and no one was going to convince me otherwise. That all changed when I received an e-mail attachment that Jane Minkley-Baker, president of the Lubbock chapter, sent about the scriptures and homosexuality. Even though I requested she send it to me after I heard her talk about it at one of our meetings, I didn't look at it for several months because I *knew* what the scriptures said—it was a sin and I didn't need to have someone else's opinion about it. After all, it would just be a matter of twisting the scriptures to say whatever anyone wanted them to say. Curiosity won out, and I finally read it. I was amazed—it wasn't histrionic, blasphemous, in-your-face, and didn't disregard my point of view. This work by The Reverend Paula M. Jackson, Ph.D., *What Does the Bible Say About Being Gay? —Probably not what you've been told* is the result of many years of Bible study and lecture presentations. "It is for people who care deeply about the Bible and hope to hear God speaking through it. It focuses on the Scriptures of the Christian Church, and the sources are the Hebrew Bible, the Greek New Testament, and the Septuagint (a Greek translation of the Hebrew Bible held in high esteem by the early church)."

It is not an easy read—and this is a condensed version of the study! If it were simple, it would be just another opinion on the subject. Instead, the author presents the facts and lets the reader come to his or her own conclusions. The entire study boils down to this one question: What if we're wrong?

The following is e-mail correspondence between Cholene and me. First, mine:

Hi Honey,

For some time I have been wondering how I can apologize to you for putting you through so much when you were

growing up. My not knowing you are gay is no excuse—as a parent and as a Christian, it was unconscionable. I have recently finished reading the draft of Ellen's memoir. As I hurt for her and what she went through as a child, I realized that although the circumstances were different, we hurt you just as much. If it were possible, I would do anything to make it up to you. I can't undo all the hurt . . . I can only do what I can to keep other kids from suffering as you did, and let you know every day of your life that you are loved, cherished, embraced for who you are.
I love you,
Mom

Cholene's reply:

Dear Mom,
First, thank you, and no apologies needed. I think Corinthians pretty much covers all of love, and I especially love the part about "now I see dimly" . . . I think of this often as we often see dimly until something shines the light. You saw dimly back then. And remember that I denied that part and prayed for healing for many years, so I wasn't too happy with myself either.

I think more than anything I had a profound sense of loneliness as a child, and that's due to a complicated mixture of things. But it is out of that loneliness and a feeling of not belonging that I gained the compassion to serve others. So it's all worked out as it should.

Once again, my precious daughter has let me off the hook.

In the spring of 2009, I began to feel that I needed to

share PFLAG with families in the Odessa area. I thought there had to be people who could benefit from it, just as I had. I didn't have a clue of where to begin. I made some phone calls, but really didn't get anywhere. I need to explain how things are in West Texas—extremely conservative. There are liberals, of course, but they are not in the majority. Not only could I not find parents of gay kids, I couldn't find any gay people! In September of 2010, Jane (president of the Lubbock PFLAG chapter) sent me the contact information for a young gay man in Odessa who had inquired about a PFLAG chapter in my area. I e-mailed him, we met at Starbucks and the ball started rolling. I have said that Jonathan was the wind beneath my wings and the thorn in my side. He really pushed me, and that's what it took to get things going. Trust me when I say that I was WAY out of my comfort zone. Cholene has often said that if you aren't living on the edge, you're taking up too much space. I've learned that being on this new "edge" is a lot more exciting and fulfilling than my comfort zone ever was.

Because PFLAG is an established, non-profit organization, it was great to be under their umbrella and not have to *re-invent the wheel*, but there was still a lot of paperwork involved. They were very kind and patient with me, walking me through every step. However, I think there was probably a groan in the national office every time one of my e-mails showed up.

Our first meeting was held in a Catholic church on December 6, 2010. Father Mark, a wonderful man, welcomed us to use one the church's large classrooms. There were about 40 people at that first meeting, plus a reporter and photographer from one of the local TV stations. I was a wreck. My stepdaughter Laron and granddaughter Susan were there for moral support. Laron told me later that Susan said, "I've never seen Grandma so nervous!" (See reference to "comfort zone" above.) It wasn't just a matter of speaking before a group of people . . . I wasn't sure if we would be safe. Unfortunately, that isn't a paranoid, melodramatic statement.

Contrary to my initial fears about the press, they were (and still are) very kind to us. I had so many TV and news-paper interviews I *almost* got comfortable with them. (There seems to be a direct correlation between a video camera placed in my face and my salivary glands shutting down. If you have ever tried to eat a peanut butter cracker sandwich without anything to drink, you'll have an idea of what my interviews were like.) The only problem we had concerning the press was due to privacy issues—the need for some at the meetings to have anonymity. Having their picture in the paper or on the six o'clock news could cause a problem at their jobs, schools, or in their homes. Confidentiality is imperative at all PFLAG meetings.

Unfortunately, that first meeting was our only meeting at the Catholic Church. The catholic bishop over this area felt that the PFLAG teachings were in direct opposition to those of the Catholic Church on the subject of homosexuality, and issued, in essence, a *cease and desist* order. Father Mark felt terrible about it, but I told him that no good deed goes unpunished. This took place right before Christmas, which was just two weeks before our January meeting. James and I were preparing to meet our kids and grandchildren in Santa Fe. It would be the first time in over thirty years that we would all be in the same place at the same time. I pulled a Scarlet O'Hara and thought, *I'll think about this tomorrow*—or at least after we returned from our trip. The Thursday before Christmas, I was to get off work at noon and we were leaving for Santa Fe shortly thereafter. I received a call from one of the local TV news stations that morning, asking if they could interview me about the Bishop's directive. I told them I was leaving town, but if they wanted to come to my house, we could do it there before I left. Our suitcases were sitting by the door when the reporter and cameraman arrived. I suspected that they *smelled* a story—hoping that there would be some controversy. (As they say, good news doesn't sell.) I told them before the interview began that this was a non-story, that we were thankful to Father Mark and his church for opening their doors to us, and that we could not have gotten PFLAG off the ground without them. The reporter was polite and kind, and even though he did his job well and asked leading questions, he didn't push or try to manipulate my words. When we returned from our trip, there was a message on our answering machine from someone at Alternative Life Solutions Counseling who had seen the interview on television, had told her boss about it, and they were offering us a meeting place. We have had our meetings there ever since. God is good!

Another serendipity that came through the press was when one of the reporters/anchors offered to speak for one of our meetings. She is a lovely young woman whose mother is gay. She told of her positive experience as a child involved in PFLAG support groups for children of gay parents. There are those who would have us believe that children of gay parents are doomed to a horrible life—I wish they could have heard her speak.

We have never had as many people at our meetings since that first one, and we don't always have the same ones in attendance—but without fail, the ones who need to be at a particular meeting, for whatever reason, are there. It may be that a guest speaker has just the right message for someone at that exact time, or it may be that there are just a few people there and someone who hasn't been able to share his or her heart at other meetings feels comfortable in doing so. When I hear the heartbreaking stories, I always think that surely the people who are spewing hate would change their point of view if only they could (or would) hear them. One of the stories was from a man in his mid-thirties whose partner died of cancer. Because he had never been able to tell his parents he was gay, and he was a professional who could lose his job if people knew, he couldn't acknowledge their relationship, and he grieved alone. There are too many stories like his.

Then there are the positive stories. A woman who was at our first meeting spoke about why she was there. She has a gay son, and although that has never been a problem to her, she was there because of all the gay teen suicides. She wanted to do what she could to keep this from happening. Adele has become a wonderful friend who has been with me every step of this PFLAG adventure since that first meeting. She is secretary of PFLAG Odessa and is a constant source of encouragement to me. Our initial reactions over learning of the sexuality of our children couldn't have been more different. Adele couldn't understand why a parent wouldn't embrace his or her gay child without reservation, and I couldn't understand how a parent could. We have learned a lot from each other. Something that is so special about Adele's story is that she is Hispanic. Typically, gay Hispanics are not accepted, let alone embraced, in their families or communities. She has given me permission to include their story:

> *"My son came home during his first year away at college and told me he had something important to tell me, and that I should sit down. I was afraid—I just knew he was going to tell me that he had cancer. He kept beating around the bush and I became more and more anxious. I finally said, 'Mi hijo, what's wrong?!' He then told me he was gay. I said, 'My goodness, I thought you had cancer or something. You don't have AIDS do you?' He assured me that he didn't. He just couldn't believe that it wasn't a huge issue with me. I said, 'Son, when you were born, I didn't receive a contract that said I was to love you, care for you, and be proud of you . . . UNLESS you were gay.'"*

Something else—Adele's extended family didn't think it was a big deal either. In our long talks of analyzing this, I learned that Adele's mother, whose husband left her to raise the four children still at home on her own, who worked three jobs to feed them and loved them unconditionally, taught them how to love by example.

I recently met Adele's son and his partner. They are delightful, bright, accomplished, young professionals. We talked at length about PFLAG in Odessa. They live in Houston and marveled at how different it is here for those in the LGBT community. They mentioned that they live in a community where there are many gay people, and they forget that not every place is like that. I thought after I left Adele's house that day that it is not much different from friends of mine who have lived outside of the United States for various reasons. Whenever possible, they find or form a "community" of Americans they can socialize with, speak English with, feel comfortable with. However, if a group of people are forced into a community of their own, that is a different matter altogether. We've seen it happen in America to racial, ethnic, and religious groups. It's wrong.

There is a wonderful group of people walking this journey with me. Through those on the PFLAG board and those who come to our monthly meetings—parents, gay men and women, a transgender person, and straight allies— my life has been enriched beyond belief. Contrary to my fears, no one has threatened my life, sent me a letter bomb, or slit my tires. I am of the impression that many who live here are tired of all the hate.

Since I have been "out," so to speak, time and again when I tell someone about Cholene I hear something like this: "You know, I have an aunt (or brother or cousin or friend) who is gay. I really love her (him) but the church says (or my pastor says or the name of a Christian leader says) that I am to love the sinner but hate the sin. And that until they get right with God and come out of the lifestyle, it's best if I just let them know that homosexuality is a sin and pray for them. That doesn't seem right, but I don't know what to do."

That "love the sinner, hate the sin" thing—isn't that just so *ecclesiastically correct?* And have you ever seen the people who tout this bit of crock *embracing,* or in any way, shape, or form, *loving* any gay people? I haven't. In fact, if they would let themselves get close enough to a gay person to get to know him or her, their thinking (and especially their heart) could be changed too. Ellen says that if a person knows one gay person, it probably won't change anything. But if they get to know two gay people, that is when change will come. I've thought about this statement and I can relate it to racial prejudice. I have heard people denigrate an entire ethnic group, but if they happen to become friends with one person of that race or nationality, they invariably say, "But they're different. They aren't like the rest of them." But if that same person becomes friends with one or more others from that group, they have to start questioning if perhaps they have been wrong.

I attended my first National PFLAG Convention in November of 2011. Aside from the marvelous camaraderie with my friends from PFLAG Lubbock, it was informative, enlightening, and I left with a resolve to make more of an impact on my part of West Texas.

Two topics stood out for me. One concerned faith and

the LGBT community. (Note: LGBT and GLBT acronyms are used interchangeably, but mean the same thing; Lesbian, Gay, Bisexual, Transgender.) A faith panel was comprised of a woman pastor, a pastor of a black church, a Catholic priest, an Imam of the Muslim community, and a Jewish rabbi (who also happens to be president of PFLAG National). It was gratifying to hear that there are those in leadership from many different faiths who "get it." The consensus of the panel was that change is not going to come from the pulpits—it is going to come from the pews. I am one pew-sitter who is not willing to keep her mouth shut any longer.

How can anyone possibly tell another person that he or she cannot have a relationship with God? One night at an Odessa PFLAG meeting, a young gay woman asked with tears streaming down her face if we could tell her of a church she could attend. We could not. It isn't only those from the LGBT community who suffer because of unwelcoming churches, but their parents suffer as well. Some of us have been going to the same church or denomination for years, but seek another church because we are afraid that our sons or daughters would be subjected to a rant on homosexuality from the pulpit. Another reason is that we parents don't appreciate the rants either. These are our children they are talking about!

To gain more information along the faith line, I attended a workshop presented by Kathy Baldock, a delightful, spunky, hilariously funny evangelical Christian who is a straight ally (meaning that neither she nor anyone in her family is a member of the LGBT community). You will find her at www.canyonwalkerconnections.com. "Repairing the Breach Between the Church and the LGBT Community" is what she is about. Her blogs and everything else on her website are interesting and informative—especially the section on scripture. I strongly urge you to take a look. Now. Put this book down, get on your computer, and start reading. (Of course, place a bookmarker at this page so you can pick up where you left off.) I admit that there was a time, not all that long ago, that if someone had told me to look at something like this I wouldn't even have pretended that I would. Try to have more sense than I had—especially if you have a gay child.

The other topic that made me sit up and take notice was The Family Acceptance Project, a community research, intervention, education, and policy initiative that is affiliated with San Francisco State University. The presenter was Caitlin Ryan, Ph.D., the project director who has devoted years to studying how family acceptance and rejection affect the physical health, mental health, and well-being of LGBT youth. Her statistics were astounding. Gay youth who were highly rejected by their families had a suicide rate more than eight times that of those who had family acceptance, and were more than three times as likely to use alcohol, illegal drugs, and to be at high risk for HIV and sexually transmitted diseases. Rejecting our kids results in a lot more than broken relationships—it is a matter of life and death. The website is www.familyproject.sfsu.edu. You owe it to yourself, and especially to the LGBT person in your life, to check it out.

Cholene recently told me of something so heartbreaking that I asked her to include it here:

> It would have taken a nuclear warhead to blast me out of the closet. I was even in the closet to myself—denial, repression, and shame are more descriptive. After I left the military and could "legally" have a relationship, it was years before I had one. And even after I was in a relationship, I was still in the closet for years after that. I attempted to blend in every way, or to avoid conversations that might require my talking about my personal life.
>
> However, as I've listened to the experiences of other gay people, one thing has become clear to me—not all of us can hide. I had a conversation recently with a close friend who is gay. He announced in a rather matter-of-fact way it had been his experience, and that of every gay male he knew, that there was a moment (usually as a young child) when it became clear to him that he was alone—no one was going to come to his rescue.
>
> He then told me his story. He was bullied as a young child for being "queer." In one particular incident, he waited in vain for his mother to do something. As he told the story, he looked out into space and said in the detached voice of someone who had perhaps resolved his profound pain and disappointment, "And then I came to the realization that she wasn't going to do anything."
>
> I put myself in the shoes of that young boy who, for reasons beyond his control, was different from the other boys. He was profoundly brilliant, had skipped two grades in school, and was exceptionally gifted musically. Under normal circumstances his mother, any mother, would have come to the rescue of a child who was in danger, either physically or emotionally—any circumstance except this

one. *The teachers, the school administrators, and even his own mother were willing to condone, and therefore endorse, his suffering.*

What message are you giving *your* child? Who is listening to what is being said in *your* home and *your* church? The following is from a precious little girl who was listening in ours:

Cholene:

I never cared whether I lived or died, so when faced with the split-second choice—save the airplane or save myself—I chose the airplane. As fate would have it, I survived and the U-2 spy plane did not. We ended up in a pool of flames about an eighth of a mile from the small, camouflaged runway in South Korea.

I have never been a "daredevil." As a pilot, I'm in the business of mitigating and managing risks. Even so, when confronted with the opportunity to take a personal risk that will not endanger others, or will shield others from danger, which was the situation I faced in Korea, I will risk my own skin. Attempting to save the plane, myself, and to keep it from crashing into others was a better option than ejecting or "bailing out."

People have characterized me as being "brave," "fearless," "courageous." I have never seen myself that way. Instead, I simply never felt that I belonged and so it was natural for me to take risks because I had rarely experienced the fear of loss—losing something that I deeply cared for. I experienced great loss with the death of my father and I survived that, but there was no one or no thing I was attached to except that airplane that night.

I'm not a psychoanalyst, but I don't think it takes a mental health care professional to figure out that my lack of "belonging" had a lot to do with the fact that I have known I am gay since I was a young child. Being gay separated me from the rest of humanity for most of my life. I felt, in a word, different, and I knew this was "not right"—not right in terms of the descriptive sense, as in a variation in nature, as well as in the normative sense— "wrong."

The not right in the normative sense came from being raised in an evangelical Christian home. We went to church twice on Sunday and once on Wednesday night from the time I was eight years old until I left home for the Air Force Academy. I added a Friday night youth service to the other three services when I became a teenager. I didn't like going to church, but I grew to love God.

Church seemed boring and fake to me. I always felt that I was less than—less than others in the church because I belonged to a blended family—the byproduct of three divorces; one on my stepfather's side and two on my mother's side. We were welcome to attend church, tithe and volunteer, but my mother and stepfather were not allowed to marry in the church, nor were they allowed to serve in leadership roles, such as board members, elders, or deacons. My stepfather was prohibited because he was divorced and remarried. My mother had an additional strike against her—she is a woman.

Even more alienating than being a member of a less than perfect "Christian" family, I was also less than because I knew I was gay. No one knew I was gay, but I did and I knew God knew. I was a fish out of the holy waters of the First Assembly of God Church. I tuned out during the services. I was present in body, but not in mind. I daydreamed about what I would be when I grew up and how I'd never go to church. When I got bored with my own imagination, I counted the ceiling tiles. I sat on the bench in my dress and leotards and itchy sweaters and Payless patent leather shoes with the buckle that never buckled well enough for me to run in, with my hair matted down with Dippity-do styling gel and I tried as best I could to pretend I was one of them. But I couldn't wait to get home to my jeans with ironed-on patches on the knees, high top tennis shoes, and hop on my Western Flyer bike with playing cards clipped to the spokes with clothespins in order to make my bike sound like a motorized vehicle. Then I would zoom off to do my "secret missions."

I spent my childhood in an imaginary world, with mostly imaginary friends. I wasn't comfortable with the real world and was not allowed to be part of the world I wanted, so I created my own. My imaginary friends and I moved from one adventure to the next, each one more dangerous and more important. My favorite adventure was to run the fences in our "working class" neighborhood with brown lawns and cinder block fences—perfect for scaling and wide enough to run on top.

My imagination had its limitations and I desperately wanted to be one of the "better thans," which in my neighborhood included my older brother Chip and my older stepbrother Phillip—the boys. They got to play on sports teams, wear uniforms, shoot guns, play war, and take their bikes on long trips across town with their friends. I was not allowed. I could cheerlead for their teams, which I did with a "bad attitude" as my brother used to say, but my permission to "play" with them was granted sparingly and on a temporary basis.

My temporary play permit was normally confined to

those times when they needed someone to play the adversary in a war or they needed a moving target. I proudly wore the uniforms of Germany, Japan, and Mexico, hoping that one day I would win—but it always ended badly for me. The cards were stacked against me. Only once did I get to be "the Americans." I was so excited at this opportunity because surely being the Americans meant certain victory. I ran into the house to tell my mom that Chip and Phillip had finally let me be the Americans.

"That's nice honey, what war are you playing?"

"Pearl Harbor!" I shouted proudly with wild-eyed enthusiasm. I did not understand the change in her expression until a few moments later when the battle began and my cut-up soda straws, little sticks and blades of grass sailing proudly in the freshly rain-filled gutter were pummeled beyond recognition by "the Japanese."

"What a minute!!!" I'm the Americans! I'm not supposed to lose!"

"Stupid, it's Pearl Harbor," my stepbrother Phillip said sneeringly.

My first reaction was, he is lying—they are lying and they have their history wrong. I ran in the house to my only reliable source of information, my mother. She confirmed it. The Americans did not always win and we suffered a horrible defeat at Pearl Harbor.

Despite my disappointment, I accepted this defeat and took some modicum of consolation in the fact that I had been allowed to be part of the war at all.

The other times I was allowed to play with them was when they needed a moving target, such as during our Ranger Rifle BB gun wars or a "smear the queer" game. BB wars are self-explanatory. Smear the queer probably needs some explanation.

Smear the queer is played with a football, preferably. It is mob versus one. The "one," of course, is "the queer." The queer catches the ball and the mob tackles the queer. I normally ended up hurt, but the pain was better than not getting to play at all. The queer position was supposed to rotate from kid to kid, except when I played and then I tended to keep the position until I got too hurt or too tired to continue.

I tried to make friends with girls, but by and large, I was bored with them and thought they were kind of mean. My interactions with them usually resulted in heartbreak. Boys could say mean things, but they didn't seem to enjoy it as much as the girls did. I was invited to a slumber party by a girl who was very popular and the prettiest girl in the fifth grade. Her mother had prepared an ice cream sundae bar for us. I helped myself. I loved sweets even more than I loved my Western Flyer. Perhaps I took more than I "needed," and the diminutive hostess of the party said, "Gee! No wonder you're so fat!" That sort of took the fun out of the night. My brothers had taught me how to take a punch and a joke, but this didn't feel like either one.

I had few friends in school, so I mostly played quietly by myself during recess, swinging or hanging on the monkey bars, unless I was forced to stay inside because I didn't finish my work. I was always late with my schoolwork. I spent the hours in school the same way I spent the hours in church—passing the time by daydreaming and reading at my own pace. I could be "disruptive" and was often given a desk next to the window in order to separate me from others so I could do my work and they could do theirs. They got their work done, but I did not. I imagined that I had a private office overlooking a beautiful city and that I was the president of a huge company and had millions of dollars at my disposal to give away to whomever I chose. I dreamed about how I would take care of my family and would buy houses for everyone and then I would design those houses on my Big Chief tablet with my #2 pencils.

My internal reality did not match the external reality. I was a chunky little kid whose mother had to plead with the teachers every year to pass me to the next grade. But as far as I was concerned, I was at the top of my game, living a thousand lives—spy, army general, entrepreneur, captain of industry, cattle rancher, famous basketball player. Looking back, I often wonder why I believed myself to be on top of the world capable of anything, despite all the evidence to the contrary. I can only come up with one reason—one source, and that is the message of love I received while trying to pass the time on those pews covered in deep maroon velour. "You are my beloved, my child." I was the beneficiary of First Corinthians, Chapter 13: Love Conquers All—even the loneliness of a chunky underachiever.

I would give anything to be able to click an "undo" button or have a "do-over." Unfortunately, there is no such thing in life. I've thought a thousand times, *If I had only known . . .* but the point is, neither we nor our church(es) had any business creating an atmosphere where she felt "less than." By my involvement with PFLAG, am I trying to do penance now for all those years of pain that I inflicted upon her? Maybe. But hopefully some other family can learn from my mistakes and *their* precious child won't grow up thinking their parents would rather he or she be dead than gay.

There is an excellent made-for-TV movie titled *Prayers for Bobby* that is based on the true story of Bobby Griffith, a young gay man who killed himself due to his Christian mother's and community's homophobia. Through her grief and remorse over her son's death, Mary Griffith, who is portrayed in the movie by Sigourney Weaver, became very active in PFLAG. I watched the movie at home one night when James was gone. I could have been that woman. Our circumstances were different, but had Cholene come out when she was a teenager, I don't know that I wouldn't have been taping scriptures all over her room and pursing my lips, letting her now how I disapproved—and of course taking her to anyone I could find who could "get her out of this." I was so glad I was watching it by myself, because I sobbed until I couldn't get my breath. It could have been my daughter who jumped off the overpass into traffic. In our discussions about suicide, Cholene has said that she wouldn't have taken her own life because of her strong faith—but that didn't keep her from thinking that if she were killed in some sort of accident, it would have been fine with her.

CHAPTER 18

Peace

After going through my "little black book" and a file where I kept notes on additions I wanted to make to this book, I decided to go over past entries in my prayer journal to see if there was anything further I needed to add. I was reading about "peace" in one of my devotional books, *My Utmost for His Highest*, a compilation of the teachings of Oswald Chambers after his death by his wife, Gertrude. Oswald Chambers was a man before his time, and right up there with Philip Yancy as one of my favorites. At the time of that reading, I had no peace. It was August 26, 2002—six weeks after Cholene's call. I had made a note of it in my prayer journal. The scripture was John 14:27 and I read these words of Jesus in The Amplified Version. *"Peace I leave with you; My [own] peace I now give and bequeath to you. Not as the world gives do I give to you. Do not let your hearts be troubled, neither let them be afraid. [Stop allowing yourselves to be agitated and disturbed; and do not permit yourselves to be fearful and intimidated and cowardly and unsettled.]"*

I then read Oswald Chambers's words—that this peace

comes from looking into the face of Jesus and realizing His *undisturbedness.* I immediately thought of the times I've been on an airplane and have become anxious over some noise I haven't heard before. I look at the faces of the flight attendants, and if they don't look worried or upset, I know that everything is all right. I am now looking into the face of Jesus to see if He is disturbed about this book we have written, and I don't see any worry lines. In the days to come, I will have to remember to keep looking at His face, not the ones that are scowling at me.

When we first started this project, I told my friend C.c. that Cholene and I were going to write our story. She was delighted and later e-mailed me that she had a vision of my speaking about it on national TV and radio. I told her I had that same vision—and people were screaming at me.

When people who knew that we were writing the book have asked how it was coming along I would say that my part was finished, but Cholene had not had time to write her part. But the thing is, *I* wasn't ready—and although I didn't know that, God did. I was still concerned about making waves and what people would think of me. I had to get to the point where, as my friend Kim would say, I could put on my big-girl panties and stand up for what I believe.

Last summer I attended my first LGBT rally. You might be thinking, "Big deal!" If you lived in Odessa, Texas, you would be thinking, "Wow! That's a big deal!" It was not only a *first* for me, but a *first* for our area. Reporters from the three local TV News channels were there. As president of PFLAG Odessa, I was interviewed and I didn't care who might catch the interview or what they might think of me. Wherever and whenever I have had the opportunity, I have been honest about what kind of a person I was and how I regret hurting my daughter. I learned later that a woman whose son is gay (and she and her husband had not been able to accept that fact) was at the park and overheard one of my interviews. She went home and told her husband what she had heard and they reconciled with their son that very weekend. I'm fairly certain that not only was Jesus not worried about what I was doing and saying that day, He was smiling.

If your world is flying apart right now, look into the face of Jesus and see if He is disturbed. I would think that He is not. The very last sentence in *My Utmost for His Highest* is, "Leave the Irreparable Past in His hands and step out into the Irresistible Future with Him."

The night I received Cholene's call, I thought it was the end of my life. Little did I know that it was just the beginning. As a friend of mine says, "Sometimes we have to let go of the life we had planned to find the one waiting for us."

AFTERWORD

Cholene Espinoza

*T*o *belong* is deeply embedded in the human psyche. The desire to be part of the whole, to love, to play, to laugh, to work together is as fundamental, in my mind, to human existence as is breathing, eating, sleeping. We, as a species, need connection. But there is a percentage of us, who for reasons beyond our control, feel, and are made to feel "separate." We are, by some, thought to be defective—by others, to be an abomination. As a gay person, I am counted in this percentage.

It is not exactly breaking news that we are often estranged from our loved ones when they learn the news that we are gay. Perhaps what may not be as evident is the fact that many of us have already suffered this disapproval and rejection—from within.

I knew at a young age that, even though I enjoyed *playing* with boys, I was *attracted* to girls—and I knew enough to know that I was better off keeping this fact to myself. I had friends in the neighborhood, but I was happier playing by myself. My best friend was imaginary. His name was Jack. We talked a lot. As I write this, I smile about Jack.

I needed a friend I could be myself with and Jack was the safest guy out there. Later in my childhood, around the age of seven, Jack moved and I met a new best friend, Jesus. I loved Jesus. He was a rebel. He was for the underdog. And he told people not to judge others. He told people the most important thing in life was to love God and love others.

My ears perked up when this message was spoken from the front of the church. It made sense to me. Best of all, it seemed as though, like Jack, Jesus didn't care that I was different. Not only that, but Jesus *loved* me. And I never felt particularly lovable until I heard about Jesus.

It was not until later that I learned most of the people in my church were more concerned with the manmade notion of personal piety than they were about Christ's message to love all and judge no one. As far as my church was concerned, it was a matter of my being a trained seal—if I *performed* as I was supposed to, I would get the *fish*. They apparently didn't understand His message: that above all things, we are to love each other—regardless of our differences.

I'll never forget when I read about Jesus washing the feet of his disciples. This stood in great contrast to any spiritual leader or minister I had encountered as a child. But I loved the idea of being helpful and caring. A friend of mine says the wounded make the best healers.

I don't remember an actual sermon being preached that homosexuals were an abomination, but I do remember seeing a movie in Sunday School about gay men in San Francisco. The movie portrayed gay people as being dangerous. Not only did homosexuals recruit, but they were violent. They would scratch your eyes out.

My only experience with an "out" gay person was a woman who came to our church a few times when I was a teenager. (Side note: This was a church decorated with pink carpeting, pink velvet cushions on the pews, and crystal chandeliers—all chosen by our male pastor who had perfectly quaffed hair and a new suit for every Sunday—however, I am not judging a book by its cover.)

This woman visited our church, but she was trying to come out of being a *Lesbian*. I was afraid of that word. I remember hearing it for the first time. Fear coursed through my veins as if even thinking that word would identify me with the "lifestyle." I still have a hard time with "that word." The woman was so nice and generous and then she just disappeared. My mother said she must have gone *back*. I didn't need to ask what "back" meant—back to the evil of the *Lesbian Lifestyle*.

I'm smiling again, sort of like when I thought of Jack earlier. Both of these notions, "Lesbian Lifestyle" and my imaginary Jack, have equal basis in reality. Being gay is not a lifestyle—no more than blue eyes or brown eyes is a lifestyle. I know this is a threatening statement, because it means that being gay is random on some level and human beings don't like random. Random means *it could happen to anyone*.

I wrote that previous paragraph with complete confidence, yet I smile again because I didn't always believe what

I just said; so I don't expect others to at first reading. It took me almost 37 years to embrace fully the fact that I am gay. Choosing the word *embrace* versus the word *accept* is critical to me. To accept means to tolerate, as one would accept the diagnosis of cancer. However, overcoming homophobia, for me anyway, is a lifelong process.

Next to telling my mother that I am gay, the most difficult conversation was with Reverend Rosemary Williams, (deceased), and her husband, Reverend Theodore Williams. Reverend Rosemary shared the vision she had for an educational center for her Katrina-ravaged community in the immediate weeks after the storm. This profoundly changed the direction of my life. Ellen and I invested and enlisted in her vision. We bought land for the center and I wrote a book that told the story of this wonderful rural Mississippi Gulf Coast community in order to help finance the center. I had already written *Through the Eye of the Storm* and had taken several trips to Mississippi to work to fulfill her vision, but Ellen and I had never told them we were a couple and they didn't ask.

As we sat in their living room, I began to cry as I tried to get the words out. The tears were mostly due to my disappointment and shame. My book had just been rejected by Christian booksellers because, while they could accept that I was gay, the fact that I was in an "active" relationship was a showstopper. Once again, being gay was stopping me from serving others.

My sexual orientation had stopped me from continuing my service in the U.S. military, as I did not want to violate

the policy of Don't Ask, Don't Tell, and now this fundamental part of my being was keeping my book, the subtitle
"A Book Dedicated to Rebuilding What Katrina Washed
Away," out of a potentially enormous market—a market we
needed. Reverend Rosemary said this news didn't change
anything in our relationship. Reverend Theodore said in the
beautiful cadence of an African American, divinely inspired
minister, "Cholene, the Bible tells us to love, not to judge."
Their words melted my shame and disappointment and I
realized that Reverend Rosemary's vision was bigger than
Christian booksellers. Today the Marsha Barbour Center,
named after Mississippi's First Lady, a woman who, like
Reverend Rosemary, also embodies the commandments to
love and serve, stands as the fulfillment of this vision.

Yet, even as I write this, Ellen and I are "in the closet"
to an adolescent from South Sudan whom Ellen and her
brother sponsored to come to the USA for a cornea trans-
plant. He was blinded when he was held as a slave in Northern Sudan. His "Master" rubbed peppers in his eyes and
hung him over a fire. Ellen and I fear that our newest family
member, based on his cultural indoctrination, might reject
us, even though we have become not only his "host" family,
but his *American* family. He needs us right now. His mother
is still in slavery and "Mama Chicken," as he calls Ellen, is
his American mother. We don't want him to lose another
mother, even if that loss is due to his own rejection of her.
So we wait until he is more secure and healthier and if
he rejects us then, we will cry and we will miss him, but he
will still be safe.

One of the favorite weeks of my life was spent caring for our South Sudanese "adopted" son. As I wrote in a piece titled *Unto Us a Child Is Born* for the Fox News Channel website:

> *Despite the trauma and loss in Ker's short life, I have never met anyone with so much joy—with so much capacity to give joy. I don't remember a time when I have laughed so much, like tonight when I served him salad and he said, "Cholene! This is for goats. Green is to wear, not to eat." Or as we were taking the clothes out of the dryer, "Oh no, please do not put woman clothes with men clothes."*

You might wonder what caused me finally, after thirty-three years on this planet, to come to terms with my sexuality.

The answer is love—or rather, the observation of love. I received a call one pre-dawn morning from a friend who is like a sister to me and her parents like another set of parents. Maria's father, Fred, had had a stroke and it was serious. I told her I was on my way. When I arrived in Denver and walked into Fred's hospital room, he looked puzzled and asked, "Cho? What are *you* doing here?" The puzzled look on his face turned to fear as he came to the realization that I was there because it was serious.

By the end of the day, we learned that within a few days Fred would need to be placed on life support in order to perform the most basic functions of survival. He didn't want that. His mind was fully intact, but he didn't want to be hostage to a life-sustaining machine.

Over the following days I watched Ruth, Maria's mother, lovingly care for Fred, and watched as Fred reciprocated this love. The love between them transcended the fear of death, the pain of pending separation, and the shock of this tragedy.

As I watched them, I couldn't help but think about the relationship I was in with a wonderful man, but a man whom I could never love as Ruth loved Fred. The problem was not with him; it was with me. I thought to myself, *This man deserves what Fred has.* Everyone deserves what Fred and Ruth have had. I realized I would never be able to deliver love of that kind and depth to a man; within a week of Fred's passing, I broke off that relationship and was for the first time honest with myself about love.

Thomas Merton says, "We find the true meaning of life through the love of another, or through the Love of God." I don't necessarily separate the love of another and the love of God, as I believe we demonstrate our love for God by loving others. Even so, there is intimate love, and intimate love is a special gift from God that cannot, as Reverend Stephen Bauman of Christ Church says, "be coerced." We cannot coerce the love of another, nor can we coerce ourselves to love another. It comes spontaneously from within. Fred and Ruth illustrated the force of this intimate love—a force powerful enough to transcend death.

As much as I want "to belong" to God and to my fellow man, being of use has always been the thing that makes me happy—to be helpful, to follow Christ's example of washing his disciples' feet, healing the sick, and feeding the poor.

I doubt I would have such a strong sense of duty to others had I not been gay. I know what it is like to be *less than,* and so it is my nature to try to build up others so they can be *better than* they think is possible. Despite my helpful nature, however, there was always a wall—an emotional wall—between me and the rest of the world. I had a secret *and* I didn't belong.

I was a military and commercial airline pilot for over twenty-two years and loved it. I was doing a highly skilled job and it didn't require the approval of human beings. Jets don't care about sexual orientation. I still love the freedom and beauty of being in the air. I especially loved flying alone or instructing. In these cases, I didn't have to talk to anyone about my personal life. Still, despite my love for flight, I had the desire to serve others in a more intimate way.

Finally, at the age of forty-five, I left commercial aviation and decided to pursue a Doctorate of Medicine. Now I am truly free. Even in my initial exposure to clinical medicine, I recognize that medicine is the ultimate social conduit. The connection to others through *service to others* is complete in the practice of medicine. Whenever a person or their loved one is sick or in pain, they want healing. They want a caring, competent, tenacious medical professional. They don't care if that professional is gay or straight.

As I read of the life and ministry of Christ, it's clear that He understood the power of healing in terms of its ability to open hearts and minds to new thought and a new way of living. The connection He sought was fulfilled through his healing. Thousands of people embraced him because He cared about their hurt, their disease, their loved one.

I hope those of you with a gay loved one will realize that we simply want to belong, to serve, to contribute, and to love in whatever capacity and with whatever gifts we have. We want a relationship with you and with God. We want to be embraced.

I will never forget the day I became a member of Reverend Stephen Bauman's Christ Church in New York City. The new members were called to the front of the church—the community. The congregation, the predominantly "straight" congregation, stood and welcomed us. They knew I was gay. They didn't care. I felt that I had finally come home, to a real home—one built on love and mutual respect and a sense of responsibility.

It is my intention to dedicate the rest of my life to serving others through the ministry of medicine. I used to pray that God would heal me of being gay. I thought it got in the way of my relationship with Him and with His creatures. Now I have no excuses. I've left the solitude and safety of the sky in order to belong, to serve and, hopefully, to heal.

Thank you for reading this book. Thank you for opening your heart and mind to us. It is my hope and prayer that you and your loved one will find richer, deeper, more authentic love in your lives—because above all things, there is love.

Acknowledgments

I have always thought the Acknowledgments section in books was comparable to an Academy Awards Acceptance Speech. Now I understand why. If it takes a village to raise a child, it takes that and more to write a book—especially one like this.

You would not be reading this book if it were not for my producers, Francesca Minerva, Ellen Ratner, and Charlene Espinoza of Changing Lives Press. (If a few of those names sound familiar I know nothing about that.) Okay, so it's nepotism. But believe me, I fit their publishing criteria as a life that was changed! They have also given me a job as an editor, thus fulfilling a longtime dream of mine.

This book was beautifully put together by book designer extraordinaire, Gary Rosenberg. I have had the pleasure of working with Gary on other projects and what he does is nothing short of miraculous. He asked me what I had in mind for the book cover. Cover? I didn't have a clue. He asked me what the book was about and I gave him a one-sentence answer. Within a very short time—like maybe an hour or thirty minutes, he sent me what you see on the front of this book. I cried. Nothing could have depicted our story any better than a soaring eagle, flying in the heavens above all things. It is said that a picture is worth a thousand words. This picture says only one: victory—victory for me, victory for Cholene, and hopefully victory for some of you who are reading this book. Carol, Gary's wife, weighed in on this idea and I felt then and still feel that it was divinely inspired. Together they make up the business team of The Book Couple. Thank you Gary and Carol, for everything.

Cathy Renna of Renna Communications is my director. Without her vast knowledge, experience, expertise and expert communication skills, this book wouldn't have made it out of the gate. You amaze me, Cathy. God must really love me to have brought you into my life at this particular time.

Cholene and Ellen had the foresight to know that a book like this was needed, and then had the confidence in me that I could accomplish it. (They have always thought I am better than I am.) My life would be so dull without this dynamic duo.

Unfortunately, the difference in my acknowledging everyone I would like to thank for helping me with this book is that I can't. Because of privacy issues that could jeopardize them in one way or another, I can't name them. Ironically, that is one of the reasons for my writing this book—that we may all see the day when this is no longer an issue. Until then, to those of you I can't name, thank you— thank you for your honesty, for your willingness to share very private moments of your life with me, for sharing your thoughts and feelings. Please know how much I love and appreciate you.

This has not been my journey only, but that of my husband, James, as well. Although we have not always been on "the same page," he has supported me in doing what I wanted/needed to do. It has been hard for me to express to him how proud I am of him for opening his mind and his heart, so I am saying it here. Thank you, James.

When I started writing this book, I needed someone who would hold me accountable, someone who knew my struggle but could be tough with me. I didn't say I *wanted* someone like that. For the first part of this book, when I was still fragile, I asked Edwina, my dear friend for over fifty years, if she would be an editor of sorts and critique my writing. I felt certain that she would be gentle and would think my every written word golden. I now know Maria Edwina Garcia Wood as "The Hammer." Just when I thought I had bared my soul and was transparent to the max, I would receive her replies to my e-mails that said things such as, "How is this going to help anyone if you aren't honest with how you *really* felt?" or "So . . . how did you *feel* about that?" I have spent most of my life hiding how I *feel* about things, so putting those *feelings* down in black and white was one of the hardest things, on an emotional level, I have ever done. It has always been so much easier to mask my hurt with humor. She saw right through it, and don't think she didn't have a lot to say about that!

After Edwina was through putting me through the wringer, I felt it safe to send the manuscript to Kim Ashby, my writing partner and great friend in Houston, Texas. I knew Kim wouldn't be gentle, but I figured there was nothing left for her to slam. Actually, I was looking for accolades. At least Edwina critiqued in complete sentences—I would get smart-aleck responses from Kim in bright red type: "??" or "Oh, please!" or "Really???" I soon discovered that if Edwina was "The Hammer," Kim was "The Sledge Hammer."

I owe you two "hammers" so much. I cringe to think of the sappy piece of drivel the book would have been without you. I love you immensely!

C.c. Nelson has read the manuscript at its various stages and has given me her thoughts and wonderful ideas for this book—and for life. Thank you, C.c., my *bosom* buddy.

I have been blessed with "balcony people" in my life—people who cheer me on, who make me think I can accomplish more than I think I can. The large supporting cast in my life has been our children and their spouses; our extended families; my grandson Justyn's other grandma (Omi), Sam Blanton; friends; coworkers (whom I count as friends); and people who don't even know me, but knew of this work in progress. I have felt your support, your well wishes, your encouragement, your prayers, and mostly, your love. Thank you—all of you.

I've said it many times, in many different ways throughout these pages, but this book truly would never have been written if God had not loved me enough to show me the error of my ways. My life has been incredibly, miraculously changed, and I am eternally thankful.

About the Authors

Shari Johnson

After ending a twenty-two-year career as a dental hygienist, Shari turned to her passion of writing for consolation, which led to an even greater passion for editing. She is currently an editor and copyeditor for Changing Lives Press.

Shari and her husband, James, have a blended family of six children—hers, his, and theirs. The family has grown to include six spouses, 13 grandchildren, and two great-grandchildren.

Shari and James live in Odessa, Texas, with their spoiled dogs, Sissy and Henry.

Cholene Espinoza

Cholene graduated from the U.S. Air Force Academy, and while in the military served as an instructor pilot and the second woman to fly the U-2 Spy plane. After leaving the military, she was a captain for United Airlines; was an embedded journalist with the U.S. Marine 1st Tank Battalion at the start of the Iraq war; and is now a second-year medical student. After obtaining her license to practice medicine, she hopes to combine her love of flying with her love of medicine to serve the people in remote areas of the world.

Cholene and her partner, **Ellen Ratner**, were married in Cambridge, Massachusetts, in December of 2004. Cholene resides temporarily in Grenada, where she attends St. George's University School of Medicine. Ellen lives in Washington, D.C., where she is bureau chief for *Talk Radio News,* a White House correspondent, and a Contributor for Fox News Channel.

Shari (left) and her husband, James, with Cholene in Grenada for Cholene's White Coat Ceremony at the start of med school, January 2011.